JACK GERNSHEIMER

THE PROCESS OF CREATING

DESIGNING LOGOS

SYMBOLS THAT ENDURE

ALLWORTH PRESS

12   11   10   09   08   5   4   3   2   1

Published by Allworth Press
An imprint of Allworth Communications, Inc.
10 East 23rd Street, New York, NY 10010

Cover design by Chris Werner and Jeff Gernsheimer
Interior design by www.partnersdesign.net
Page composition and typography by Sharp Des!gns, Inc., Lansing, MI
Cover photo by Chris Werner

ISBN-13: 978-1-58115-649-2
ISBN-10: 1-58115-649-9

LIBRARY OF CONGRESS CATALOGING-IN-PUBLICATION DATA
Gernsheimer, Jack.
Designing logos : the process of creating symbols that endure / Jack Gernsheimer.
       p. cm.
Includes bibliographical references and index.
ISBN-13: 978-1-58115-649-2 (alk. paper)
ISBN-10: 1-58115-649-9 (alk. paper)
 1. Logos (Symbols)—Design. 2. Industrial design coordination. I. Title.
NC1002.L63G47 2008
658.8'27—dc22
2008016921

Printed in Thailand

CONTENTS

PREFACE

Since I began designing logos in the mid-1960s, there have been many times when I've wished for a concise reference for the designing, caring, and feeding of logos. Logo designers, whether aspiring or active, need an information source to go to for facts relating to logos and the logo design process. This is not a book about branding; there is more than an adequate supply of those. This is not a book of rules and regulations on the development of full-blown corporate identity campaigns, although many aspects of corporate identity design are discussed. This is not a book featuring a gallery of this year's award-winning logos. What this book should be, I decided, is a sourcebook of information that deals specifically with the design and implementation of the logo: A place you can go to convince a reluctant client that what you are presenting is valid and carefully thought out and developed. A tool to help assuage the concerns of the decision maker and to help him get his associates and fellow workers to not only accept the new mark, but enthusiastically embrace it. A source of information that will assist the designer not only in developing the mark itself, but in presenting enticingly, and even defending, the logos being presented. While there are varying interpretations and uses of these words, within this book, I use the word "logo" to describe a symbol, mark, or icon. I use the term "logotype" to refer to a word or words that accompany or replace the logo as an identifier.

When my twin brother Jeff and I left the advertising and design world in New York City in 1968 and ultimately settled on a farm in rural Pennsylvania in 1971, very few people besides those in the field of communications knew what the word "logo" meant. In 1974, my three-year-old daughter Jessica was a clear exception to the rule. Jeff and I had been working extensively on a promotional campaign for a group of newly constructed apartment buildings. After many alternatives were considered, we named the complex "Twelve Trees," after a suggestion offered by a friend who was familiar with an Asian proverb of the same name. The logo, if you will, was actually a photo of three tree lines with a large orange circle behind them. As I was taking a sunset drive, I heard a small voice from the backseat excitedly say "Daddy, look, your logo!"

Over the course of my studies and practice in graphic design, a period I refer to as "lucy ollo to lorem ipsum,"* not only has most everyone come to know what a logo is, but about twenty-eight million of them consider themselves logo designers. Any PlayStation jockey worth his salt has designed a logo for this band or that school project.

*In the late sixties and early seventies, press type was used extensively on comprehensive sketches, or "slick comps," as they were called. Blocks of gibberish, usually starting out "lucy ollo," were commonly used to represent "greeked" type. Years later, greeked copy is digitally available in preset text starting with the words, and referred to as, "lorem ipsum."

ACKNOWLEDGMENTS

Where better to start than to thank the two people most instrumental in my ability to write this book—my father, Solly Gernsheimer, and my mother, Hilde Gernsheimer. Whether or not they agreed with every educational and career choice, they always respected my judgment and assisted me in the pursuit of my aspirations. Through school to the School of Art at Syracuse University, to J. Walter Thompson in New York, and ultimately to Partners Design, the support given by my parents never wavered.

I thank Dr. M. Peter Piening, my professor at Syracuse and my mentor at J. Walter Thompson, for giving me the courage to aim high and for helping me appreciate the elegant simplicity of most classic logos. On that note, I thank Paul Rand, Herb Lubalin, Tom Geismar, and the masters of logo design mentioned in the pages of this book, for blazing the trail and establishing lofty standards to aspire to meet. These designers understood the ultimate benefit of continual refinement to the essential core, so that the final mark not only communicated but also illuminated the message.

Thanks to the many fine associates and interns who worked side by side with me at Partners Design: Jason Wister, Justin Wister, Joanne Shipley, Sean Costik, Teresa Van Wagner, and Jason Dietrick, to name a few. The exchange of influence was mutually beneficial, and together we made each other better designers. A special thanks to Chris Werner for continually pushing the envelope, and for designing the beautiful cover of this book. Thanks to Lindsay Krapf, Brianna Kelly, and the other interns who assisted me in this project. Thanks also to Nicole Potter, Kate Ellison, Bob Porter, and Tad Crawford of Allworth Press for their support, encouragement, and assistance. A big "takk" to Bruno Oldani, Rainer Jucker, Harald Gulli, and Heinz Finger, my fine and brilliant friends who made my 1978 experience in Norway a rich one, both artistically and personally.

Thanks to the business associates, friends, and family who lent many a hand along the way. Thanks to Dick Whitson, an inspirational designer I had the pleasure of working with at Armstrong for many years, and to others, including Reed Dixon, Alan Weinberg, Peter Horvath, Barbara Morrow, Rob Fitzpatrick, Bill Fitzpatrick, Steve Wilton, Lauretta Dives, Amy White Berger, Sharon Gernsheimer, Peter Marshall, Andy Lackow, Jessica Battaglia, Albert Boscov, Chip Kidd, Jamie Greth, Bill White, Earl Houser, Jan Gernsheimer, Bradley Gast, Susan Homan, Jane Palmer, Bill Kreitler, Rudy Mosteller, Sandy Solmon, Donald Blyler, Ray Deimler, John Hummer, and Steve Cicero, to name but a few.

A very special thanks to my wonderful wife, Nancy Wolff, whose artistic eye, exquisite taste, and loving heart combine to make me both a better designer and a better person.

Last, but not least, my most heartfelt thanks to my loyal partner, identical twin, and best friend, Jeff Gernsheimer. Over the years I've watched him transform from a wildly enthusiastic student of design into a design director of the highest order. Jeff understands the words of his mentor, Earl Houser, who made him aware that successful design must do more than look good; it must work hard to communicate its message. Every piece of work credited to me in this book bears Jeff's influence, and without his outstanding knowledge of the art and profession of graphic design, my work would be greatly diminished.

Enjoy.

Everywhere you look today, you're bombarded with logos. Logos on the Web, logos on cars and trucks, logos on TV, logos in newspaper and magazine ads, logos on billboards, logos on shoes and clothing, and on and on. Logos are nothing new. In fact, logos have probably been around since humans first needed a way of distinguishing one person's belongings from another's. What is new is the degree of proliferation of logos in every facet of our society. And they're not going away.

As you might expect, with all the logos out there, it's becoming more and more difficult to design one that stands out from the rest and promises to endure over the years. How do you go about creating logos that work on all levels, when it seems like it's all been done? How do you design logos that will still look good in twenty-five years? Good news: It's very challenging, but it's not impossible.

The first section of this book discusses the myriad aspects of logos. From their historical development and their place in society, we move into a very detailed discussion of the logo design process. Section 2 is a timeline of classical logos, dating from the eighteen hundreds to the present. Here we take the opportunity to review these marks in an effort to determine why they have endured—in some cases, for over a century. Finally, the last section gives us an insight into the design process of many successful logos. We'll observe the evolution of these marks from the initial idea to the final version. We'll take the opportunity to dissect not only the mark chosen, but other designs that are not selected but worthy of consideration.

Designing Logos: The Process of Creating Symbols That Endure looks at the process of logo design and the criteria used to determine whether or not a logo stands a good chance of being here down the road. Whether you're an educator, a student of design, a CEO recognizing the need for a corporate identity change, or just a fan of strong design, this book will help you make a more well-informed decision about the quality of logos.

"If, in the business of communications, image is king, the essence of this image, the logo, is a jewel in its crown."

PAUL RAND

DESIGNING LOGOS

| # LOGOS THROUGH THE AGES

01   02   03

THE ROAD FROM PREHISTORIC MARKINGS TO THE MODERN-DAY LOGO IS A LONG

AND WINDING ONE. From markings on cave walls to the cylinder seals of Mesopota-

mia, to ancient Egyptian and Chinese symbols, to brands burned into the coat of

animals, to Greek monograms, to the markings of Roman and German bricks, to the

heralds, hallmarks, and stamps of medieval Europe, to Italian watermarks, to the logos

of the modern era, symbols have been developed and refined to facilitate identification.

01   02   03   04   05   06   07   08   09   10

AN ANALYSIS OF THE EARLIEST MARKINGS MADE BY HUMANS SUGGESTS THAT

IMAGERY HAS BEEN USED TO IDENTIFY OR INDICATE OWNERSHIP SINCE

THE BEGINNING OF RECORDED HISTORY.

EARLY SIGNS OF IDENTIFICATION IMAGERY

Logos, in one form or another, have been a fixture in humanity's environment for ages.

Cave paintings date from early Paleolithic (35,000 B.C.) up to Neolithic (4000 B.C.) times. *Homo sapiens* have been adorning walls and other surfaces ever since. Early markings appear to have used charcoal and pigments. The images often represented animals and objects, such as the sun, that exist in nature.

As time went on the images became simpler and more stylized, giving them a degree of distinctiveness. By the end of the Paleolithic period, some of the images began to resemble what would come to be known as letters. There's a theory that early precursors to written language were developed in order to identify the contents of sacks and pottery containers in which food was stored. The markings were often impressed into small clay tags. The amount contained was also indicated by what looks like a primitive numbering system. It's possible that the system was decimal-based because man has ten fingers on which to count.

As villages formed and people lived together, it became necessary to identify and confirm ownership. Potters marked their vessels, and this allowed those producing higher-quality items the opportunity to sell more product because of their superior reputation. Around 3000 B.C., Mesopotamian cylinder seals were used to authenticate and seal documents. Symbols were etched into the surface, and when rolled over a damp clay surface, the "trademark" was raised out of the clay. This method of identification made the image very hard to duplicate, which thus all but assured authenticity.

EARLY LETTER FORMS

The Egyptian system of writing with pictorial images lasted from 3100 B.C. until around 400 A.D. The Chinese also contributed to early writing and identification. Their calligraphy was first used around 1800 B.C., with characters supposedly inspired by the footprints of animals and birds. The characters, known as logograms, were symbols that represented an entire word. Over the centuries, the Chinese created paper and devised ways to print on it. In the third century A.D., seals were made by carving characters into hard surfaces such as jade, ivory, silver, and gold. These were then used as stamps for identification purposes.

Some Roman bricks from the first century A.D. bear identifying marks impressed into their surface. Later, from the twelfth through the eighteenth centuries, German stonemasons used a system of identifying their work based on a special grid from which to derive their personal mark. The *Mutterfiguren*, or "Mother marks," appeared to be based on that grid.

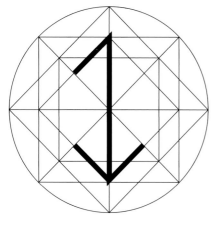 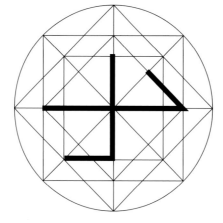 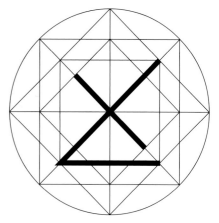

The word "brand" derives from an Old English word that meant "to burn," and it came to mean a mark that was burned into the skin in order to signify ownership. For over four thousand years, brands were used to identify cattle. Brands have also been used on humans as recently as 1822. There are depictions of branding on the walls of Egyptian tombs dating back to around 2000 B.C. The use of fire-heated irons was preceded by less permanent pine tar and paint. Later, brands were sometimes replaced by the more humane earmark, which was a stamped piece of metal clipped to the animal's ear, but branding—searing in the mark as a means of identification—is still being practiced today.

THE EMERGING LOGO

The term "logo" dates back to ancient Greece, and it literally means "name," although it became associated with symbols and trademarks. Early Greek design included the development of monograms, first with one letter, then two or more letters intertwined. Reference to monograms goes back to the first century A.D., when they often served as the signature for illiterate signatories. Since some authorities suggested that monograms be recognized rather than read, they truly became direct forerunners of the contemporary logo. In the case of royal monograms, the letters were often topped with the image of a crown. Royal monograms symbolized authority on items such as coins, buildings, clothing, and banners.

Ceramic artists designed identifying symbols that were usually impressed into the bottom of a dish, vessel, or other item prior to firing. The mark then served as a permanent identifier of the author of the piece.

HERALDRY IDENTIFIES COMBATANTS

The herald was the individual responsible for identifying knights taking part in combat tournaments. The existence of a herald at a battle was first recorded in 1173. The herald determined the legitimacy of a combatant by judging the authenticity of the heraldic marks, since the participant wore protective armor that all but concealed his identity. Sometimes known as a coat of arms, the identifying symbol was often worn on the coat. Another name for the shield or crest is the escutcheon. These symbols were also used as a stamp

TOP, LEFT: One can find heraldically influenced logos being used by many colleges and universities. Although secondary imagery within the symbol includes books and more obscure items, the shield is still commonly used as the containing shape that holds those elements. These logos generally have an air of authority and legitimacy to them, and many have endured for several decades. Their longevity is generally more attributable to their established status than to great design.

TOP, RIGHT: The Fust and Schoeffer logo was first used to identify the work of German printers in 1457. The symbol appeared in a book of psalms printed in Mainz, Germany, known as *Mainz Psalms*. The Greek letters *chi* and *lambda* appear in the mark, along with three stars. The symbol is still in use today.

BOTTOM: Rud Rasmussen's furniture, designed by Kaare Klint, was identified by this classic logo, created in 1930 by Gunnar Biilmann Petersen. In addition to the symmetrical reflection of the initials, there is an implication of precision and balance.

applied to heated sealing wax to secure correspondence, as carvings on tombs, and as banners carried into combat or flying at the family estate.

The herald was responsible for resolving issues related to coats of arms that looked too much like one another. Today, a similar practice is used to determine if a new logo is too similar to an existing one, but it's not the herald that upholds the standards but lawyers and the U.S. Patent and Trademark Office. Coats of arms have extended from family identifiers to towns, cities, and states. They are sometimes used in contemporary logos as well, although usually in a simplified and stylized fashion. Later, coats of arms sometimes took the shape of a lozenge rather than a shield when used by non-combatants.

HALLMARKS AND OTHER STAMPS

In London, objects made of precious metal were often stamped with an identifying mark at Goldsmith's Hall, which is why the stamp became known as a hallmark. These marks served as a guarantee of the metal's purity. The manufacturer of the article has, since 1863, been identified with a stamp known as the sponsor's mark. Early examples of punch marking metals actually exist from the Byzantine era around the fourth century A.D.

European furniture makers routinely stamped their product with an identifying mark, often in the form of a paper label like the one shown here.

Printers also identified themselves with logo-like marks. Johann Fust and Peter Schoeffer were the first printers to use a trademark (shown here) to identify their work.

By impressing a mark into paper while it was wet and in the mold, paper manufacturers applied a subtle stamp that permanently marked the paper. Known as watermarks, these marks were used in Italy as early as the thirteenth century. They are still being used to identify high-quality paper products today. Variations of the orb and cross symbol, which resembles an upright Nabisco logo, were often used by printers to identify their work. The use of such symbols associated the printer with Christianity because of the incorporation of the cross. Specific letters and shapes distinguished one mark from another. Over the years, much more elaborate imagery was used for printer identification.

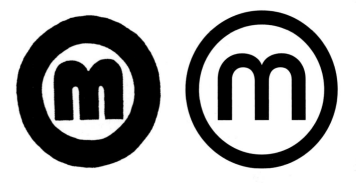

One can clearly see the influence the Wiener Werkstätte trademark might have had on the Volkswagen logo designed in 1938. The logo designed by Lucian Bernhard for Manoli cigarettes appears to be another harbinger of things to come, ushering in the age of minimalist logos. Designed in 1911, it would appear to have had an influence on the contemporary logo for Muzak designed by Pentagram in the late 1990s.

THE MODERN ERA

The Wiener Werkstätte, the workshop in Vienna that was contemporaneous with the British Arts and Crafts movement, was founded in 1903. One of its goals was to remove "useless decoration" from contemporary design. Trademark and monogram design was moving into the twentieth century with a belief that geometric purity and simplification was the order of the day. This attitude was exemplified by members of the Vienna Secession: those artists who, in the late nineteenth century, resigned from the "official" arbiter of aesthetics, the Association of Austrian Artists.

INTERNATIONAL IMPACT

European influence on contemporary American design was heightened by the immigration of designers, many escaping political oppression, in the 1930s. Among them were Herbert Beyer, Will Burtin, and Herbert Matter, themselves influenced by the modernism of early twentieth-century European design. Matter, along with Eliot Noyes and Charles Eames, collaborated with American designer Paul Rand on the development of the Westing-house logo (see page 104), which has become a true classic.

In his 1947 book *Thoughts on Design*, Rand (born Peretz Rosenbaum in Brooklyn, New York) said the designer, in an effort to create the abstract, expressive symbol, "reinstates his problem in terms of ideas, pictures, forms, and shapes. He unifies, simplifies, eliminates superfluities. He symbolizes . . . abstracts from his material by association and analogy."

Highly regarded design critic Steven Heller has said of Rand: "He was the channel through which European modern art and design—Russian Constructivism, Dutch De Stijl, and the German Bauhaus—was introduced to American commercial art." Rand's influence on contemporary logo design is apparent not only within the pages of this book but also in the visual landscape at large. It would be difficult to spend a day in America and not encounter the work of this design master.

Logos have become increasingly important in the commercial world as companies struggle to distinguish themselves from one another in the global marketplace. Because commerce crosses international boundaries, logo design is becoming more and more global in its scope. Not only are logos legally required to be cleared for use domestically, they must also distinguish themselves from marks used in other countries.

These tracing paper sketches were done in 1991 by Jack Gernsheimer. As the designer, I developed a logo for Scott Paper's environmental education program encouraging adults to teach children about renewable resources such as trees. Here, small sketches initially were done, followed by larger ones, offering a closer look at the final alternatives. Another design, of a hand holding a leaf, was developed for the client's consideration.

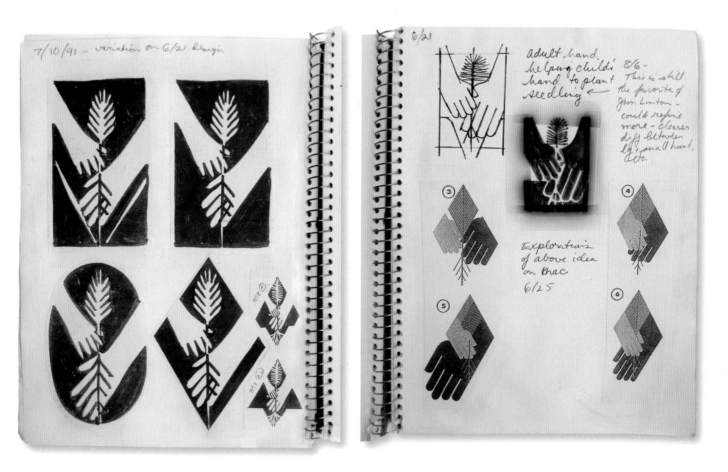

7/10 - w/ Jamie Scott -
go back to 6/21 design and work from
that starting point.

7/16 - 7/18 (on NYC bus)

The shrinking planet syndrome, as it impacts logo design, is both a good and a bad thing. The global exposure of digital images makes it increasingly important that a logo distinguish itself from others. This becomes more difficult as new logos enter the commercial arena daily. On the bright side, the cross-cultural influences of international design introduce new aesthetic sensibilities and expand the design vocabulary of designers more than ever before.

TOOLS OF THE TRADE

Although the process of designing logos has remained similar, the materials used to assist in logo design have changed dramatically over time.

EARLY MODERN LOGOS

Years ago, logos were often designed by a printer's apprentice or a sign-shop employee with an artistic flare. There was no assurance that the person charged with this task was equipped to develop a symbol that effectively carried the heavy weight imposed on a logo. By the same token, many fine marks flowed from the brushes of gifted sign painters or the quills of multitalented pressmen. As recently as thirty years ago, most people not involved in some capacity of marketing or advertising did not know the meaning of the term "logo." Gradually, as the demand for unique logos swelled, so did the ranks of graphic designers who were all too eager to try their hand at logo design. A few got it; most didn't. For every good logo that's been designed, there are a number of mediocre ones, and one or two disasters. Once again, the old bell curve applies.

The tools used to assist in the design of logos have certainly changed over the centuries. When printing became a common form of communication, icons began to find their way onto the page, often making a clear and strong impression, both literally and figuratively, first with black ink and then with multicolored inks.

GRAPHITE AND INK ON PAPER

Pens and then pencils served for many years as effective tools for developing all sorts of designs, including logos. As paper became more commonly available, it was the preferred

material for sketching and developing ideas. As various papers with distinctive characteristics and qualities were developed, some were shown to facilitate the design process more effectively than others, and thus emerged as favorites within the design community. Key among them was a category of paper of varying thickness, color, and transparency generally referred to as "tracing paper." Because tracing paper is not opaque, one could sketch an idea and then place a piece of tracing paper directly on top of the original sketch and make adjustments, continuing the refinement process indefinitely. If the designer thought to number the sketches, he or she could observe an interesting and often fruitful sequence of evolving marks, leading to a logo he deemed worthy of the client's consideration.

A favorite writing tool, the pencil began to offer a broadening range of leads, from soft to hard and thick to thin. Later, pens and pencils held inks and leads with a wide variety of available hues, thus allowing the designer to introduce color to the exploratory process.

Final art, or "mechanical" art, usually involved rendering the mark in pen and ink. After the "ruling" pens came rapidographs of varying thicknesses to assist in this process.

MARKERS, PAINT, AND COLORED PENCILS

Around the middle of the twentieth century, a favorite tool of many designers was introduced. Known generically as "magic markers," these felt-tipped pens offered a clean, neat, and simple way to apply rich color to the sketchbook page. They had nibs of varying sizes and shapes, typically offering either a thick or thin line option. Later, markers were manufactured with both thick and thin tips for greater range of use. Numerous manufacturers offered a wide range of colors, from pastels to deeply saturated hues.

Not so many years ago, comprehensive sketches, known in the industry as "comps," were developed to show the client, as closely as possible, the appearance of the final printed logo. Earlier comps were often painstakingly painted, typically with gouache. Later, they were often illustrated with markers. Others rendered in colored pencil on the paper, which was then often mounted on a piece of white illustration board to provide rigidity and a greater perceived value. In certain instances, a product known as a "color key," developed by 3M, was "burned," showing the design on acetate in a limited variety of colors. While neat and helpful in presenting designs, this process had obvious limitations.

PRESSTYPE, COLOR TRANSFERS, AND PHOTOSTATS

In the sixties, a product often referred to as "presstype" was manufactured by Letraset, among other companies. This item consisted of a font family applied to a translucent substrate. Each individual letter was positioned and transferred to the paper below by rubbing on top of the character. While this procedure provided a way of neatly showing a wide variety of fonts and sizes, it had limitations. The alphabets were usually black, white, or one of a very limited number of colors, and usually had only one point size per sheet. The sheets were expensive, the number of letters per sheet was finite, and the page was often retired with a plethora of *q*'s and *x*'s and a dearth of vowels.

Following presstype, along came a similar but much-improved product often referred to as "INTs," "matrocolors," or "identicolors." The transfer process was the same as that of presstype, but the information on the page was custom created to the designer's specification. This allowed the logo, logotype, or other graphic element to be depicted in the correct color or colors neatly, accurately, and appealingly. It was, however, a time-consuming and costly process, and thus was used sparingly.

Final art, or "mechanical art," often involved photostats, which were adhered to illustration board with rubber cement or hot wax.

"Slicks" or "repro sheets" were provided to the client with the logo printed in a range of sizes. The chosen logo would be cut from the sheet and integrated into the ad or other item being printed.

MEET YOUR NEW BEST FRIEND

Arguably the most significant tool developed to facilitate the design of logos, as well as a myriad of other applications, was the personal computer. No single product introduction has come close to having the impact that the computer has had on the development of logo designs.

What some claim to be the first "personal computer," known as ENIAC, was introduced in 1946. The "Electronic Numerical Integrator and Computer," designed at the University of Pennsylvania by John Mauchly and J. Presper Ekert, was originally built to calculate artillery firing tables. While this behemoth took up 680 square feet, weighed nearly thirty tons, and used over seventeen thousand vacuum tubes, it blazed the trail for the development of today's personal computers. By the 1970s, smaller computers were being developed specifically for design generation. Early models, however, such as the Artronics computer, were high in cost, operated painfully slowly, and had very limited capacity. In 1976, Apple brought out its first microcomputer, and in doing so set forth a sea change in the way designs were to be produced. The software manufacturer Adobe was a major contributor to that change. Launched in 1987, Adobe emerged as the premier developer of graphic design programs, most notably Illustrator and Photoshop. With these arrows in the quiver, the logo designer was equipped to build, step, and repeat a logo indefinitely. Like the tracing-paper logo that preceded it, once in the system, the digitally generated or scanned logo could be copied and refined with relative ease.

COMMON MISCONCEPTIONS

The assumption that the development of logos using computers is virtually effortless is, of course, dead wrong. There's still a great deal of time required to design a great logo, whether it is done digitally or, in rare cases, conventionally. More importantly, technology is no replacement for talent. No matter what the tool, a skilled designer will find ways of designing logos that possess the strong qualities needed to work effectively. As much or more time goes into creating a logo digitally as into designing a logo conventionally because designers often take advantage of the opportunity to dig deeper and look at more of the countless options available to them. The ability to explore limitless alternative designs can actually become a problem unless the designer exercises restraint and recognizes the point at which further exploration becomes self-indulgence.

As was often the case in precomputer days, final art incorporated photostats and a product known as Amberlith® or its darker cousin, Rubylith®. The "liths" were orange or red film on an acetate substrate. The film adhered to the acetate, and was cut with an Exacto® knife. Then, some of the film was peeled off the base, and what remained served as either a positive or negative film.

In the case of the GeriMed logo, designed by Jack Gernsheimer in 1985, pencil lines were drawn and notes writ-

ten regarding which oval templates to use in which locations. The lines were then perfectly drawn in ink on a translucent sheet of vellum placed over the enlarged stat seen here, using the templates. The final drawing was cleaned up and photostated with reverse film, resulting in a positive image of the finished logo.

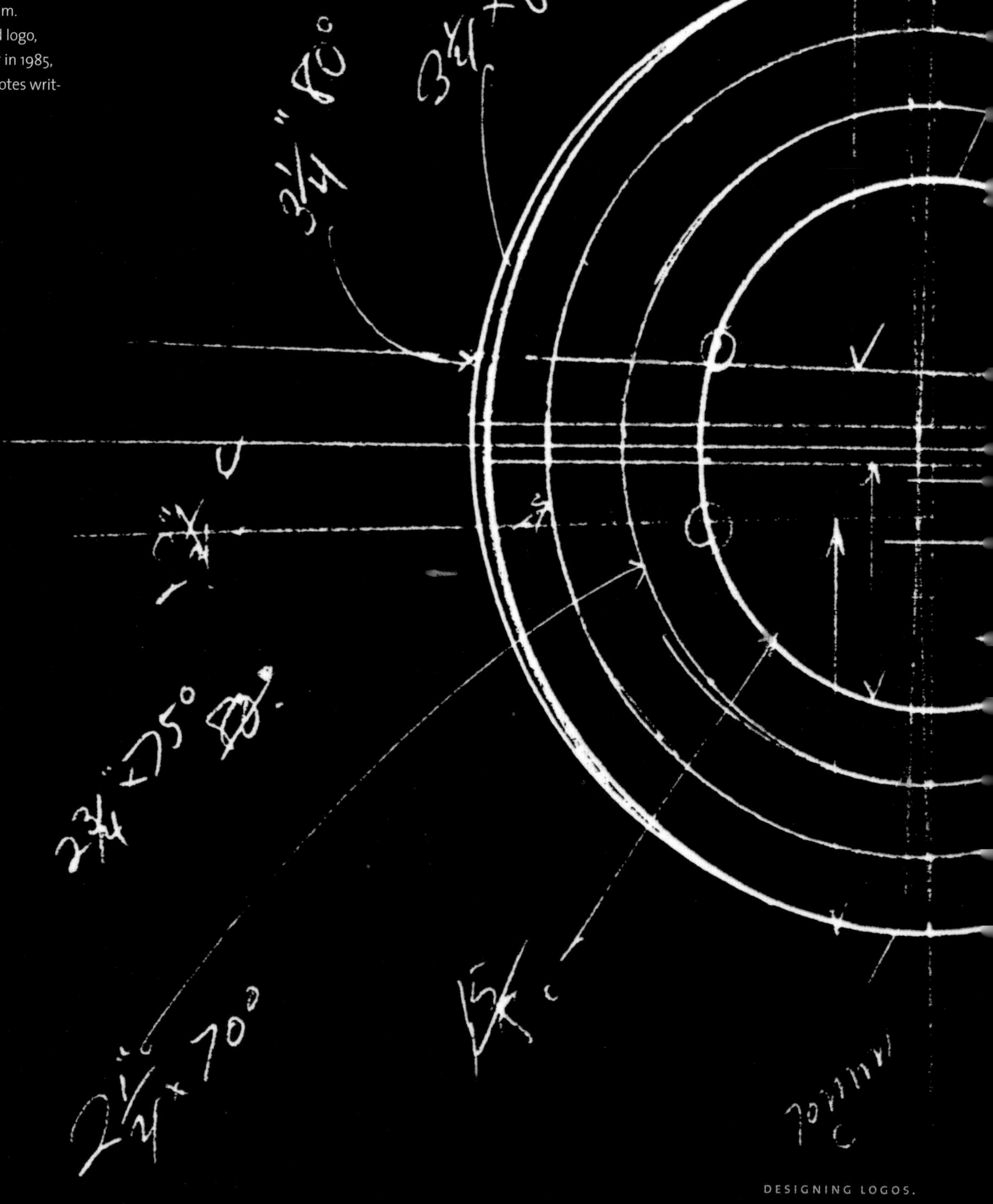

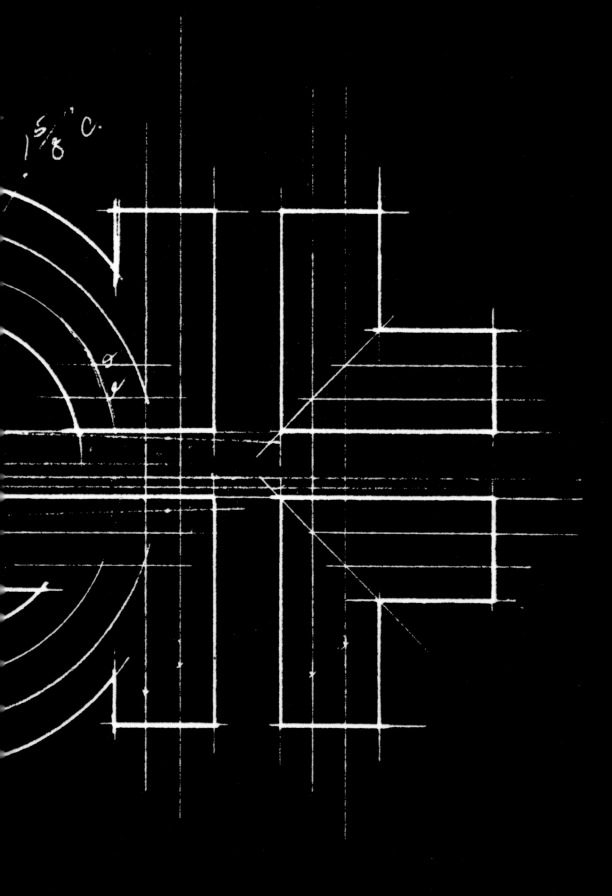

SEAMLESS INTEGRATION

One aspect of computer-generated logos most appreciated by designers, particularly those who remember practicing before the digital revolution, is the ability to seamlessly take the logo from design exploration to final printed product. Years ago, the logo would be designed, selected alternatives would be worked up, and then the options would be presented. Once the client selected one or two for refinement, new comps were made and presented, along with a proposed adaptation such as a letterhead, envelope, or business card. Upon acceptance, the logo, along with other applications, was built mechanically, usually with pen and ink on illustration board, Amberlith film on acetate, and black-and-white photostats. Type was either hand drawn or specified— "specked"—and galleys were delivered from the service bureau. Mechanical art was produced by pasting up the elements precisely onto matte-coated white illustration board with tape, wax, or rubber cement. Rules would be hand drawn in ink with a ruling pen and, later, a rapidograph pen.

The boards, once complete, were placed behind glass on the copy board of a large camera and photographed. From the resulting negative film, printing plates were burned and wrapped onto one of the drums on the offset printing press. Ink was mixed and the job was printed. Prior to offset, letterpress printing was typically done. This process used metal type and "electros," which were etched metal slugs of the logo composed into the page. The metal surfaces were inked and pressed onto the paper, leaving the right-reading impression on the selected stock.

Thanks to digital technology, the process of logo design, from beginning to end, has been simplified considerably. The logo is often designed, refined, finalized, and printed from one file in seamless fashion. Various digital printers output imagery of all sizes on countless substrates. As a result, the logo can now be seen adorning tractor trailers, banners, signs, and even the sides of multistory buildings.

BEWARE THE SEDUCTIVE MONITOR

One pitfall to be aware of is the seductive nature of the monitor. As monitors become lighter, bigger, flatter, and clearer, one can observe the slightest details magnified dramatically. With millions of available colors, great magnification power, and bright illumination, it's easy to forget that the logo on the business card will be small, nonilluminated, and made up of four or fewer colors. Even more challenging, the logo may be used in a want ad, poorly printed in black on low-quality newsprint at a size of one-half inch or less. In a sense, designing for this worst-case scenario can help avoid serious production problems down the road.

Another concern that needs to be addressed is color fidelity. The print-oriented logo is designed on a computer, and color is developed to look its best on the designer's monitor. After that, a test print is often run. Sometimes the client will look at a PDF (portable document file) and then run off a color copy on his printer. The printing house charged with producing stationery will proof the color and, upon approval, run the job. With each step and adjustment, the color may vary more greatly from the original appearance of the logo on the designer's monitor. It's critically important to be vigilant about color consistency as the process unfolds. The logo should have the same appearance whether it's on a Web site, business card, or fifty-three-foot trailer.

As was the case with the tools that preceded it, the computer can be invaluable if used efficiently by a skilled and knowledgeable designer who understands the unique demands and challenges of the art of logo design.

01   **02**   03   04   05   06   07   08   09   10

LOGOS PLAY AN INCREASINGLY IMPORTANT ROLE IN THE IDENTIFICATION

AND PERSONALIZATION OF PRODUCTS, SERVICES, AND ORGANIZATIONS.

WHAT MAKES A LOGO GOOD?

Today, many people think of themselves as designers, regardless of the amount or quality of the training they've received. In years past, the process of designing, "comping," "specing," and producing mechanical art for a logo was typically done by someone skilled in the process. This didn't insure a good end result, but it did limit the number of people who designed logos professionally. With today's technology, the production steps are much more integrated and therefore accessible to both skilled and unskilled designers alike. That means the buyer—in this case, the client—must be aware of the background and skills of the designer he hires. Logo design is a specialty, and like other specialists, be they nephrologists, third basemen, or pastry chefs, the bell curve applies. There are always a few practitioners who should not be practicing, those whose work ranges from mediocre to good, and a handful of those who almost always do outstanding work. Even great designers have their specialties and limitations, and logo design is a specialty few designers excel in.

Why? Because a good logo effectively distills a great deal into a concise symbol that is ideally attractive, cohesive, conceptual, distinctive, enduring, legible, memorable, relevant, sophisticated, and versatile: the ten characteristics of a well-designed logo. That's a tall order for the little fella, and few hold up to those high standards. But the greater the number of these characteristics inherent in the mark, the more likely it is that it will hold up over time.

TEN CHARACTERISTICS OF A LOGO THAT ENDURES

Following are ten criteria by which to judge logos. The more that apply to the logo in question, the greater its likelihood for success and longevity.

WHAT MAKES A LOGO *DISTINCTIVE*?

A logo should have an appearance unlike that of other logos. Ideally, the distinctive logo will stand out in a crowded field by virtue of its unique appearance. A distinctive logo may, and probably will, have an appearance that is in some way similar to imagery that has preceded it, but it will have an essence all its own, separating it from the pack.

Some examples of logos that possess this quality are

The 1994 logo for Chevy's Impala is a standout in terms of sophistication. The lines are fluid, powerful, and efficient, with just enough information to define the leaping antelope. In contrast, the naïve, albeit charming, deer logo for a music recording label inspired by the mythology of the Huichol Indians suggest that the company has a friendly, homespun quality.

The flowery logo, reminiscent of art nouveau of the early twentieth century, used for a Midwestern funeral parlor is an example of imagery that may have appealed to folks when the company was founded in 1936, but it has a dated, stuffy, and uncomfortably morbid appearance today. The choice of burgundy and dark green does nothing to brighten the somber element.

those of Woolmark, GE, and IBM (see pages 111, 101, and 117). Each of these classics has its own distinctive look and is immediately recognizable.

WHAT MAKES A LOGO *SOPHISTICATED*?

Not always, but 95 percent of the time, clients want their logos to reflect a sense of good taste and sophistication. When that is the case, the avoidance of inappropriate imagery, fonts, colors, and motifs is key. A sophisticated logo exercises restraint and reduces adornment and activity to the essential visual information necessary to simply and clearly communicate its message.

By the same token, a sophisticated logo and a stuffy logo are not one and the same. Stuffy logos lack a pleasing air and can be unnecessarily somber. Selection of a font or color palette that is inappropriately conservative can undermine the success of the mark. The use of imagery that is inherently or stylistically solemn or even uncomfortable, such as a casket for a funeral home, is ill-advised.

WHAT MAKES A LOGO *CONCEPTUAL*?

When a logo contains elements born of intelligent thought, it adds a positive dimension that, once recognized, gives the mark a greater sense of conceptual sophistication. Smart logos suggest smart companies, products, and services.

A good example of a logo that integrates a conceptual component is Cubic Metre (see page 114). By simply turning the lowercase *m* ninety degrees, rather than doing the obvious and using the numeral *3*, the mark becomes more distinctive, memorable, and visually interesting.

The Lithografix mark, at first glance an unusual letter *L*, beautifully communicates that it represents an offset printer because of the halftone impression being transferred from plate to substrate (see page 117). Many conceptual logos take time to reveal their secrets, making the discovery all the more gratifying for the beholder.

WHAT MAKES A LOGO *RELEVANT*?

When imagery relevant to the product, service, process, or entity is selected or developed, either photographically or illustratively, the logo relates more clearly to that which it

represents. The inclusion of one or more relevant visual elements, providing they don't undermine the simplicity of the logo, adds layers of secondary information about the entity. Multiple levels of information, if effectively integrated, can make the mark richer and more visually interesting. Even if the secondary image is discreet and not easily detected, eventual detection will have an effect similar to the exposure of hidden information, enriching the logo once it is revealed.

Keep in mind that there may be a potential downside to the infusion of relevant imagery into the mark. If the company expands into new sectors, the logo could be rendered obsolete if the visual element is too specific to the initial product or service. For example, which broadcast company logo expands easily into the music realm, ABC (letters in a black circle) or CBS (eye)? Right you are. The eye is a great asset in the TV sector but is a liability in the recording world. That said, unless there's an expressed reservation about "pigeonholing" the mark, incorporating appropriate imagery to reinforce the symbol is better than intentionally striving for ambiguity.

WHAT MAKES A LOGO *VERSATILE*?

Whether the logo is applied to a sixty-foot-high oil tank or a ballpoint pen, it should read well.

If type or elements within the logo close up when the logo is reduced or break up when it is enlarged, you will have problems. In some cases, a revised version of the logo is needed for reduction beyond a certain point. Additionally, a revised "reverse" version of the logo is sometimes necessary. In any case, a logo that reduces, enlarges, and reverses well is desirable.

Logos are likely to be reproduced in many ways and in many materials, including metal, wood, glass, plastic, or cut vinyl for signage; on paper for printed materials; and electronically for use on the Web and with other digital media. A tough but important test for today's logo is its ability to shrink down into the URL field, where it will appear when the Web site is being visited. Not only is this symbol shown in full (RGB) color, it's about one-eighth inch in height.

WHAT MAKES A LOGO *COHESIVE*?

If you feel the need to draw a box, circle, or other shape around the logo, chances are the design lacks the cohesive

PHOTOS BY JEFF GERNSHEIMER

quality that visually contains a good mark. As a rule, the symbol should not require an additional containment element to hold it together, although there are logos that are designed to be kept within a box, circle, or other shape.

If, however, that shape was not intended to be used but seems a necessary addition, it may be prudent to revisit the design and be sure there is a sense of cohesion. All too often, the designer or her client is too quick to include an exterior device to hold the logo together. In many cases, further exploration will yield ways to contain the mark in a more integrated way.

When elements within a logo appear detached from one another, the logo tends to look fragmented and disjointed. A good logo has a sense of cohesion, holding it together visually. This applies to the symbol, the type, and their relationship to one another, as well. Too much leading in a multiline logotype can make the word look less strong. The same holds true when there is too much space between the letters of a logotype. Here, however, there is a broad exception. Widely kerned type often works very effectively in a logotype, providing it is stylistically appropriate and thematically compatible.

One way to improve a logo's cohesiveness is to reduce the space between elements, provided those spaces hold open when the mark is reduced to a small size. The designer must determine the right balance of proximity and separation from both a visual and a reduction standpoint. Caution must also be taken to ensure that the elements within a logo don't run together when the mark is built with pixels on a monitor, particularly when viewed in low resolution.

Interweaving is another way to hold together the elements in a mark. In the case of the PACA logo shown on page 24, the letters, instead of not touching, overlap and are interwoven. By doing this, the individual components in the mark seem bound together and provide a sense of unity and interaction. The WiTF logo, shown on page 25, employs a slightly different method to hold the characters together. While not interwoven, the letters overlap one another. In doing so, there is a sense of cohesiveness suggesting strength, not only within the mark but in the entity it represents, as well.

Two logos that are contained in a black square represent PACA (Picture Archive Council of America) (see page 184) and WiTF. As the designer of both logos, I first built the marks without considering the box. Once the letters were in place and the colors developed, I felt the letters would pop more against a black, rather than a white background. Observation confirmed the assumption, but I needed to ensure that the black background would be a permanent part of the mark. The square was the logical shape to use, because both logos had nearly square letter clusters. The size of the outer square was determined by visual examination, avoiding too much or too little breathing room for the inner letters. One issue that needed to be resolved was how the black box works against black. Rather than having a white outline, the standards call for a reduction from 100 percent black to 80 percent black in the square.

The logotype for Micro Center, a chain of electronic merchandise stores, exemplifies compromised legibility. The letters *M*, *R*, and *T* are particularly challenging to read. There are a total of four ligatures that do little to improve the situation. Derived from a font that could be classified as futuristic, this logotype trades legibility for attitude.

MICRO CENTER

WHAT MAKES A LOGO *ATTRACTIVE*?

Now we're getting into the realm of subjectivity, which is more difficult to quantify. That said, some things are more universally appealing than others. Take, for example, a movie star. Had you polled one hundred men in 1960, asking them if they found Elizabeth Taylor attractive, the likelihood is that ninety-five would have said yes. The point is, there are things of beauty that have broad, if not universal, appeal to viewers. While cultural influences may have a bearing on this, the goal is to design a logo that has visual appeal to the greatest number of viewers possible.

It's been said that symmetry is one of the characteristics that makes a person's face attractive. While that is not without exception, it may be a safe generalization. Of course, other factors play into the equation, such as skin condition, bone structure, and the like. The same could be said of logos: If all things are equal, symmetry does contribute to beauty. Other factors include composition, proportion, and balance.

WHAT MAKES A LOGO *LEGIBLE*?

Particularly in a logotype, or when type is prominent in a logo, legibility is important. The more easily readable the letters or words, the clearer the message. While it's tempting and often desirable to customize letters and create ligatures, care should be taken to keep the logo as legible as possible. Sometimes ligatures improve the readability of the letters, but often the physical linking of two letters makes them read more poorly. Making letters bolder can cause the counter, or inner area of letters like *e* and *o*, to close up. In general, customization improves the logo and logotype, providing it's done well and with a light touch.

Legibility doesn't apply only to the readability of type. If an object is being introduced to the logo and no one can identify that object, you've got a legibility problem. If it's a car, a four-year-old should be able to identify it as such. If objects and words don't read quickly and easily, they should be refined until the situation is rectified.

The Mobil logotype was designed around 1964 by Chermayeff and Geismar (see 111). In contrast to that of Micro Center, this classic endures because of its elegant simplicity and uncompromised legibility. Additionally, the red *O* gives the logotype distinctiveness and immediate recognition, even from a great distance.

WHAT MAKES A LOGO *MEMORABLE*?

If properly designed, a frequently seen logo will be readily recalled by a viewer. A mark that is simple in its construction, though not necessarily in concept, is generally easier to recall. This is advantageous when building and maintaining brand loyalty. Recognizable silhouettes can facilitate easier identification because the viewer is given a cue at first glance. It's been said that you could recognize the old Coca-Cola bottle from a mile away (provided you had great vision or a good pair of binoculars). That's because the silhouette of the bottle was so distinctive and original.

Another test of recognition and memorability compares the late Cingular man, "Jack," with the Nextel logo. Chances are, you can more easily conjure the former than the latter, largely because of the logo's profile and general simplicity of detail.

The advantage of having a memorable logo is obvious. Memorability breeds familiarity, which in turn establishes a comfort level, building a sense of trust. In cases where money is involved, increased sales are a by-product of strong branding, and a memorable logo is a key factor in a strong brand presence.

WHAT MAKES A LOGO *ENDURING*?

Last, but not least, a good logo must stand the test of time. Unlike an ad or brochure that may have a shelf life of six months to three years, the logo should work for decades. Your client will be investing too much time, money, and effort getting their visual identity up and running to want to start the process again in ten years. The idea is to build equity by keeping the logo in the public eye as much and as long as possible. Changing the logo frequently diminishes the equity that has been built. On the other hand, refreshing and slightly modifying the logo on a periodic basis is sometimes advised. When this is undertaken, losing as little equity as possible is desired, so infusing the look and spirit of the original logo into the refreshed one is important. If, however, the logo is designed to endure at the outset, the need for periodic refreshing is reduced.

The best way to ensure the longevity of a logo is to stay away from trendy imagery, fonts, and colors that tend to date the logo. You don't want the viewer, professional designer or not, to say that logo was designed in 2002 because there are characteristics that give away its age. Remember the spate of logos that had full or partial orbits flying around letters and words? How nineties was that?

There are in fact inherent contradictions when holding logos up to the ten-characteristic challenge. For example, most long-lived symbols are essentially simple, yet with simplicity comes the likelihood that other symbols resemble it. When it comes to memorability, how can a logo for Ore-Ida potatoes stand toe to toe with Nike? In one case, we rarely if ever see the mark, while in the other, we see the logo daily because tens of millions of dollars have gone into building the hugely successful brand. It's hard to watch a sporting event today without having the Nike logo constantly flashing before our eyes.

The effectiveness a branding campaign achieves has a direct bearing on the way a company or product is perceived.

This makes objective assessment of many logos difficult. Nevertheless, a logo can still be graded for its success, recognizing that such an analysis remains somewhat subjective.

SECONDARY CHARACTERISTICS OF A GOOD LOGO

In addition to the ten primary characteristics of a good logo, there are secondary ones, as well. They include being multicultural and having the ability to be animated.

Years ago, international commerce was practiced by a relatively few multinational companies. A handful of financial powerhouses, some European auto manufacturers, and a few large oil companies come to mind. In today's global marketplace, international trade affects us all. Most of the products we buy are manufactured outside the United States. We export and import millions of products daily. With this international trade comes a greater need for international communications.

The more broadly a logo can be understood, the better. The use of universally recognizable imagery, such as that used to facilitate international travel, helps to enhance the level of understanding a symbol achieves worldwide.

Given the fact that most logos today find themselves part of interactive media, the ability to animate the logo effectively is a bonus. Restraint and good taste should be applied when setting the symbol into motion. A logo appropriately animated can add visual interest and a dynamic quality. By the same token, if a mark bursts into flame, spirals down a drain, or explodes into a thousand floating chards of color, it should be for good reason. A poorly animated logo can contaminate and degrade the environment in which it is placed, leaving a negative impression and undermining the perception of the brand.

STUDYING THE CLASSICS

There's no better way to inform oneself about outstanding logo design than to look at the classic logos, many of which have endured and remained appealing and effective over many years. These are the marks we've lived with, often for decades, and continue to relate and respond to. They tend to adhere, in varying degrees, to the objectives that define a good logo.

It must be acknowledged that objectivity with regard to

recognition is skewed because we are exposed to some logos much more frequently than others. While acknowledging that these ratings, particularly in the category of attractiveness, are subjective, the ten-characteristic rating system will give us a general sense of the strength of these logos.

THE CORNERSTONE OF THE BRAND

It's important to keep in mind that the logo can't do everything. It would be great if every logo somehow had all the pertinent information visually inherent in it. That way, we all could look at it and immediately know who it represented and what they do. This is, of course, unrealistic. But keep in mind that the logo doesn't appear in a vacuum. It's seen in ads, on facility signage, on stationery and business cards, and in many other applications and environments that clarify who or what it represents. It won't be left out on its own until it's a big boy or girl. Until then, at the very least, it will be accompanied by a parent or adult in the form of a logotype and possibly a tagline or descriptor.

However, a logo is almost always an integral part of the larger branding picture. The logo is, in fact, the cornerstone of the branding campaign, no matter how extensive or modest the effort. It is the visual element that the viewer most often sees, and therefore it most directly influences her impression of a product or service.

Let's say Joe represents his company at a trade-show booth, and he meets a potential client. His company may be a multimillion-dollar corporation, with hundreds of employees, offices scattered around the globe, huge manufacturing facilities, hundreds of products, and so on. Still, the first thing likely to influence Joe's potential client's impression of his company will be him, his display environment, and his business card. His business card may be the only thing the potential client takes away from the encounter. If the card, and particularly the logo on the card, is well designed, it will suggest that Joe's company does things well. If, on the other hand, the card and logo are poorly designed, illegible, and unattractive, the impression it leaves will be, whether consciously or subconsciously, negative.

Let's consider two retail giants, Target and Sears. What is the first thing that comes to mind when these two names are mentioned? Most probably, it's the Target logo. Even though Sears has been around seventy-six years longer, the simplicity of the Target logo, not insignificantly supported by millions of dollars of brand reinforcement, largely in the form of television advertising, has made Target a highly recognizable as well as a highly regarded brand. And each time the logo is seen, it reinforces the impression of the viewer, be it positive or negative.

In addition to using the logo in store-identification signage, Target uses the logo in many interesting ways. It can be seen in a repetitive pattern on bags and in various ways on product packaging and in TV commercials, trucks, ads, and countless other applications. What is seen throughout the branding campaign is that the logo stays intact and consistent, and whatever is designed seems to be designed well.

WHAT'S APPROPRIATE?

A well-designed logo is the key component of a visual identity program, but it's only the first step in the process of developing a new or refreshed campaign. Once the logo has been designed, much work must be done to insure that the logo's application is handled with the same degree of care and consideration as the logo design itself. There are an infinite number of approaches that can be taken when applying the logo to various items. Depending on the client, a designer can take a very straightforward and conservative approach or a radical, unorthodox approach to the application design process. The likelihood is that the logo should and will be adapted somewhere between those extremes. Several variables determine the right degree of distinctiveness with which the logo should be applied to items such as business card, letterhead, environmental graphics, and more. Who is the client and what is its personality? What message is it trying to impart when the viewer sees its materials? Is the primary audience conservative, radical, or mainstream? How much is the client willing to spend for the design of a business card that's out of the ordinary? How important is it to wow the card's recipient? What expectations do the recipients have, and will they be troubled by a departure from their expectations?

Let's take, for example, a law firm or a medical practice. For decades, it was considered inappropriate, even unacceptable, for lawyers and doctors to advertise. While it's now common practice, a high degree of decorum is expected, thus suggesting to the designer that a conservative treatment for the stationery may be advised. But even within these professions, there are variations in the appropriate degree of style and distinctiveness. For example, designing a corporate identity program for a New York City entertainment law firm allows for a more stylish look than a program for a criminal law practice in Toledo. The dermatologist or plastic surgeon in Los Angeles can appropriately make a more stylistic statement with her business card than the neurosurgeon in Topeka. It's the designer's job to consult with the client, view the competition, access the market, recognize budgetary limitations, and determine the right approach to the development of print and interactive media.

Monetary considerations will also have a bearing on how much time can be allocated to post-logo design applications. It can be very helpful for a designer to offer more- and less-expensive application design alternatives. That way, the client can decide where to place greater resources, whether in the development of an interior and exterior signage system, for instance, or in the design of business cards and letterhead.

Determining which items are most important to the overall branding effort will help prioritize which items should be given most attention by the designer. For example, if a company has a relatively small sales and service staff and a large fleet of vehicles, the lion's share of the effort and budget should obviously go toward the decoration of the "rolling billboards" rather than to the stationery items. As a result, while keeping a holistic perspective on the overall project, the vehicle design should precede and ultimately influence other applications.

Keep in mind that a poorly designed logo, beautifully and consistently adapted across a visual identity campaign, may well be more impressive than an awesome logo weakly and inconsistently applied to components. Of course, one should strive for nothing less than the ideal combination of a great logo brilliantly applied.

01 02 03 04 05 06 07 08 09 10

GATHER AS MUCH INFORMATION AS YOU CAN ABOUT THE ENTITY FOR WHICH

YOU WILL BE DESIGNING. THE MORE YOU KNOW ABOUT THEM, THE MORE LIKELY

YOU'LL DESIGN A LOGO THAT REPRESENTS THEM APPROPRIATELY.

While gathering lots of information may seem excessive, the more you know about the product or service you're designing a logo for, the better equipped you'll be to develop a logo that is appropriately representative.

In addition to interviewing the client directly, it's important to look for other sources of information about the entity the new logo will represent. Going online is a good first step. Visit the client's Web site and see where that takes you. The fact is, you should begin gathering information on the client before your first meeting together. When setting up an initial interview, it's good to request that current literature and information be sent for your review. This also gives you the opportunity to see what's been done in the way of design, which could indicate a look that appeals to the client. On the other hand, if the client is looking for a new designer, he may not be pleased with the "look" the brand currently has.

It's comforting for the client to know that the designer took the time to learn about the company. The information you gather can help you ask the right questions and be up to speed when the interview begins. This tells the client you're interested in the client's business. It looks good to have a highlighted printout of some Web pages sitting next to your notepad as you enter the meeting; clients will appreciate the fact that you made the effort to read and note things about them. While online, you can search for articles and other information about the company, its competitors, its associates, and its clients. You can also gather offline sources of information, including printed items such as a company capabilities brochure, pamphlets, newsletters, and annual reports. Product literature such as sell sheets, ads, brochures, and packaging will help familiarize you with the client and the company's needs.

INTERVIEWING THE CLIENT

The first thing most designers want to do, after hearing initial details of a logo design project, is fire up the Mac, double click the Illustrator icon, and get down to it. Usually, ideas begin percolating well before the client has finished his introductory comments on the nature of the project. Acknowledging that early design ideas can be fresh and unlabored, a quick and simple sketch can help jog the memory further down the road in the design process. That said, the first order of business for the logo designer is not cranking out designs. Rather, he or she should be listening intently while jotting down notes and parenthetical thoughts as the client goes into as much detail as possible about the logo design project at hand. Along with the note taking, it's your job to ask all the relevant questions you can think of. Rather than being put off, most clients are pleased with your desire to learn more. After all, the more you know about them, the more likely the logo you design will properly represent them. In fact, it's very helpful to jot down some questions even before the initial meeting begins. Even better, a well-prepared and attractively designed questionnaire can make a positive impression and yield helpful information.

Following are some questions that might be asked of the client:

1 YOUR CURRENT LOGO

1.1 Do you have an existing logo and/or logotype?

1.2 If so, approximately how long has it been in use?

1.3 Why have you decided to review your current identity system?

1.4 Are you inclined toward a total, major, or minor redesign of your present logo?

1.5 What are the qualities you like about your present logo?

1.6 What, if anything, do you dislike about your present logo?

1.7 Have you been using more than one logo or logotype concurrently?

1.8 Do you feel there's a good deal of equity in your existing logo?

1.9 Can you provide us with examples of your current literature, etc.?

1.10 If your company were a car, what model would it be?

1.11 If your company were a car, what model would you like it to be?

2 YOUR EXPECTATIONS

2.1 What do you expect of your new corporate identity program?

2.2 Have you observed logos that appeal to you? If so, which ones, and why?

2.3 Have you observed logos that don't appeal to you? If so, which ones, and why?

2.4 If available, can you provide a Web address to facilitate our review of those logos?

2.5 Please list images that come to mind when you think about your industry.

2.6 Is there something inherent in your process or product that suggests imagery that can be integrated into the logo design? A piece of equipment, a step in the manufacturing process, etc?

2.7 Are there any colors or other characteristics you like or dislike?

2.8 Please indicate, on a scale of 1 to 10 (highest), which characteristics should apply to your new logo:

A sophisticated	I complex
B lighthearted	J masculine
C reserved	K feminine
D lively	L strong
E progressive	M placid
F traditional	N powerful
G dynamic	O responsible
H simple	P friendly

3 YOUR COMPETITION

3.1 Who do you consider your main competitors?

3.2 What do you think of their logos?

3.3 Are you impressed with their promotional literature?

3.4 Do you think their Web site is effective?

3.5 Can you provide us with Web addresses or other applications?

3.6 Can you provide us with examples of competitors' literature, etc.?

4 FACILITATION

4.1 Please rank the following applications of your new logo in order of importance. Typically, the more public exposure, the more important the item.

A vehicles

B business cards and stationery

C your Web site

D product literature

E product packaging

F trade show display

G point-of-purchase displays

H exterior and interior signage

I additional environmental graphics

J annual reports

K billboards

L ads

M apparel

N other

4.2 Do you want to implement a full identity modification or a selective one, or simply introduce a new or "cleaned up" logo?

4.3 Is there an event or target date when you'd like to introduce your new program?

4.4 Would you prefer to roll out your entire new program at one time or as items such as business cards need to be replaced?

THE MORE INFORMATION, THE BETTER

The more you know about the entity the new logo will represent, the better. Who are the most important viewers of the mark? Who are the second- and third-tier viewers? Prioritization is important because you want the primary recipient to be spoken to most directly. In other words, a logo for a philanthropic fund may be directed toward contributors, recipients, financial personnel, school administrators, community leaders, local media, and the general public. The logical primary viewer of the fund's logo is most likely the contributor, because without their involvement, the funds aren't there. In such an instance, ask the client to describe the demographics of the typical—if there is a typical—contributor. How old are they? How educated are they? How sophisticated are they? Describe the various funds involved in the program. Are they diverse or similar in nature? Are they primarily given in the form of scholarships? How does one qualify to receive assistance? Is there a typical recipient? If so, find out as much as you can about them. All these factors will play into your approach to logo design later on.

HISTORICAL INFORMATION CAN HELP

Other information that will be helpful includes details about the entity being represented by the logo. Get as much historical information as you can. While much of the knowledge you gain will not directly affect the logo, it will provide good information to keep in mind. It may surface during the design process and suggest imagery or motif options. In theater, an actor often draws from historical knowledge of her character even though it may not seem relevant to the current character. This technique can offer a subtextual understanding of what made the character who she is today. This can apply to design as well, as you study historical information that informs and influences the final logo design. Is the company a start-up, or has it been around for a while? If it has been around, how long? Has it evolved over the years, or is it providing the same basic product or service it did early on? Does it have an existing logo? If so, why is it being redesigned? Is there much equity in the old logo? If so, how much should you stray from the established look as you work on the redesigned mark? Does the entity enjoy a good reputation? Are there established colors or fonts that should be retained?

Ask the client to describe in as much detail as possible the nature of the product or service they provide. What do the products look like? How have they been promoted? Who are the competitors? Are the competitors more or less established than your client? Are the products or services the competitor provides very similar to your client's? Are your client and competitors competing for the same dollars? How do the competition present themselves: their literature, their Web sites, their business cards, their advertising, their product designs, their packaging, their point-of-purchase materials, their environmental graphics, their uniforms, and their vehicles? Gathering information from and about the competition can be very helpful in familiarizing yourself with the industry and varied approaches others have taken to promote themselves. Visit their Web sites and request as much literature as they will send you.

GET FIRSTHAND INFORMATION WHENEVER POSSIBLE

Another important way to familiarize yourself with your client is to tour the facilities. Not only will you see how the client's current logo is being used, but you can get a sense of

While touring Carpenter Technology Corporation in 1995, I was given a firsthand look at the multifaceted process of converting the ingot of steel into a spool of wire. After the steel was stretched and thinned to the desired gauge, the red-hot coil was left to cool. The recollection of that image directly influenced the final logo design.

where and how the new logo might be integrated into the environment. You're also seeing the facility with a fresh eye, so unlike the executive showing you around, you may well see things that could be helpful in the design process but which would not have been discussed in the interview: a piece of equipment, a step in the manufacturing process, a product prior to transformation. Is there something inherent in the process that can suggest imagery that can be integrated into the logo design?

While designing environmental graphics for a new facility of a manufacturer of textile braiding machines, my brother Jeff observed a series of blueprints of old machinery the company had manufactured. By touring the building, he uncovered beautiful imagery that he then incorporated into the new program. The blueprints were cleaned up, greatly enlarged, and applied directly to the reception-area walls. The color contrast between the walls and the graphics was minimal to avoid overwhelming the viewer, particularly those who worked there on a daily basis. Had Jeff not taken the time to walk around and familiarize himself with the company, great graphic imagery would not have been woven into the facility's interior.

WHAT APPEALS TO YOUR CLIENT

It is sometimes helpful to get a sense of the client's likes and dislikes when beginning a logo design project. Asking them to gather work that appeals to them, whether related or unrelated to the project at hand, may give you an insight into their aesthetic sensibilities. Is there a common denominator in the visuals they show you? Are there certain similarities? What can you glean from these works? The knowledge you gain from this exercise can prevent you from pursuing a path likely to be rejected early on, whether the rejection is justified or not. For better or worse, taste plays a part in the selection of the logo you'll be designing. Why waste precious time and money working on one or more alternatives that will be summarily rejected because the client doesn't like green, or type on a curved baseline, or extended sans serif fonts. While the client's taste should not be the primary determinant for selecting a logo design, taste will play a part in the decision making process, like it or not.

LOOKING FOR CUES

In the process of gathering information, listening is an important component. The accomplished musician applies a discerning ear in order to hear and understand the nuances inherent in a fine performance, and in doing so, prepares to incorporate into her interpretation of the work that which she finds appealing and appropriate. The writer gathers information from many sources, then prioritizes, organizes, and edits the information before presenting it in his own distinctive voice. Likewise, the astute logo designer goes through much the same process, but with an eye, as well as an ear, peeled for cues that may be helpful once the design process begins. By continually looking for imagery appropriate to the project at hand, the designer not only looks at that which obviously applies but—equally important—that which is more subtle and less obvious. In doing this, the designer builds a reference bank of imagery that is likely to result in less clichéd, more novel, and unexpected end results.

ESTIMATING THE PROJECT COST

Having gathered much information about the new project, the designer is now in a better position to estimate the cost of, as well as design, the corporate identity program. If you are expecting to be paid three times as much as the client has budgeted, you're both likely to be unhappy.

One of the ironies of logo design is that you may be spending close to the same amount of time working on a design for a large client as you will working on a design for a small client. Nevertheless, the amount you can charge for the design of a logo is very likely to differ. While that may well be the case for the logo itself, it's less likely to apply to items designed after the logo has been developed. For example, designing the application of a logo on a golf shirt, unless a novel treatment is pursued, is a fairly simple task that should take the same amount of time whether the client is large or small. What will differ, however, is the amount of time spent on a standard letterhead design versus a unique design. While the former should take no more than a couple of hours, the latter could take days, because the options are limitless.

LEARN ENOUGH TO QUOTE ACCURATELY

In order to provide a reasonably accurate estimate, you will need to ask the right questions and gather the right information. On what will the logo be placed? The basic American package of items typically designed includes a standard 8.5" x 11" letterhead, a #10 standard business envelope, and a business card. Beyond those items, there are numerous materials that may or may not be included in the adaptation process. Various forms, including fax cover sheets, transmittal forms, invoices, notepaper, stickies, and personal stationery are likely to be needed in a larger company. A variety of envelopes, including window, personal note size, 9" x 12", and others, may also be needed. The client may need you to design interior and exterior signage and environmental graphics, vehicles, premium items, and articles of clothing. Brochures, product literature, packaging, and point-of-purchase materials may all need to be quoted. Web site design, from a simple home page to a highly complex e-commerce site, will also factor into the overall cost of the project.

DON'T OVERWHELM THE CLIENT

In order to avoid scaring off a client, it's best to break the estimate into phases. Begin with the all-important design of the logo itself. The number of alternatives you present will determine the number of hours you spend on this first phase of the operation. In the simplest of possibilities, determine how much time you are likely to spend preparing one design for presentation. There's an obvious upside and downside to this scenario. While this offers no alternatives from which the client can choose, it does provide the client with a logo that is relatively inexpensive to develop. As for the developmental time needed to produce the logo, experience matters. A graphic designer who has specialized in designing corporate identity systems for many years is likely to zero in on viable and nonviable design directions quickly. Chances are, over the years, that designer has learned what does and doesn't work, and she will be inclined to stay away from designs that will ultimately present problems. A new designer with little or no experience designing logos may well pursue paths that lead to problematic solutions or dead ends.

ESTIMATING IS NOT AN EXACT SCIENCE

When estimating the amount of time the logo design process will take, it may be necessary to account for inexperience by reducing the hourly rate or the number of billable hours the less experienced designer will charge the client. By the same token, a highly experienced and skilled logo designer can bill more per hour because he or she will probably develop viable alternatives in less time. Either way, the adjusted price should be fair to the client and the designer. In the end, what the traffic will bear will affect the price as well. It's not uncommon to spend twice as many hours refining a logo design as you are able to bill. Unless you get the client's permission to add to the estimated cost, be prepared to work at the reduced hourly rate. In the end, your integrity as a designer and businessperson is of the utmost importance.

HOW LONG DOES IT TAKE?

How many hours does it take to design a logo? It depends on the graphic designer and his approach to the project. How many designs will be developed? How fully will the alternatives be developed? How skilled is the designer? How experienced is the designer? These and other factors all play into the amount of time needed to design a logo.

When scheduling the initial design presentation, first find out how truly pressing the job is. The likelihood is that the client will be eager to get things moving and will want to see initial designs as soon as possible. While trying to accommodate your client, be realistic about the time it will take you to thoroughly explore and develop the logo alternatives you plan to present. If the budget is tight, you'll have less opportunity to delve as deeply into the exploratory process; consequently, you may need to turn out the initial phase in a couple of weeks, schedule permitting. Of course, you always have the option of investing more time in the project than you'll be getting paid for. You're likely to find this the rule rather than the exception. Because you care deeply about the quality of the works you create, you may find that full remuneration is of less importance to you than artistic integrity. While this can be a noble and worthy attitude, try to avoid having people take advantage of you.

On the other hand, if you choose to design a logo for an organization or cause you feel deeply about, donating some or all of your time can be a very rewarding experience, yielding results that are beneficial to your development as a designer and to society in general. Symbols that are well designed can greatly facilitate cross-lingual and cross-cultural understanding in ways that words simply can't. To paraphrase a familiar adage, "A well-designed symbol is worth thousands of words."

In the best and most gratifying case, your work can play a part in breaking down barriers of communication and understanding, and in doing so can promote a higher degree of concern and cooperation between people in need and people in power.

EXPERIENCE *DOES* MATTER

Back in 1972, I designed one of my first professional logos, and largely due to my inexperience, I struggled for weeks trying to develop an appropriate identity for a group of four family-owned Boscov's department stores (see pages 38–39). Finally, at about four o'clock on the morning a presentation was due, the logo leaped off the sketch-pad page. I was so relieved and exhausted that I wept as I joyously refined the sketch, with tracing paper over tracing paper, to a stage worthy of presentation.

Once this design appeared, my first concern was that I might have seen it used by another company. This is not an uncommon concern, particularly if the design is a simple one. We are bombarded with symbols daily, and one can be subconsciously influenced without trying to imitate a previously seen mark. Fortunately, there was no resemblance to an existing mark, and the 1972 Boscov's logo was embraced and used extensively for twenty-seven years.

Now, from the vantage point of a designer with hundreds of logos under his belt, I believe I would need to spend considerably less time on the initial concept and design phase of the process. On the other hand, the refinement and final art construction time necessary for some logos is only somewhat—not significantly—reduced with added experience.

OVERLOOKING THE OBVIOUS

As it happens, I was given the opportunity to refresh the Boscov's logo some twenty-seven years later, when the chain had grown to nearly forty stores. This time around, because of my design experience, the redesigned *B* in the circle was taken directly from the customized script. By doing so, the compatibility of the logo and the logotype was perfect. That was not the case with the initial script, which predated the 1972 logo and was frustratingly and problematically incompatible with the mark (see pages 58–59 in chapter 5).

Keep in mind that a less-experienced designer may be more inclined to take risks that may result in a less conventional approach, while the more experienced designer may gravitate toward the tried and true. These are, of course, generalizations that don't always apply.

SEEK INSPIRATION (CAUTIOUSLY)

A favorite professor of mine at Syracuse, M. Peter Piening, was a man many years my senior. He once told me that when he was stuck in the process of designing, he would go to the Sears catalog, close his eyes, open the book, and place his finger on the opened page. He would then open his eyes and see the closest thing to where he was pointing. Having done that, he would begin to make connections, no matter how obscure, between the object on the page and that entity for which he was designing. Once this process was initiated, a more liberated approach ensued and the creative logjam began to dissipate.

Using a strategy similar to the Sears catalog exercise, I have on numerous occasions gone to a *Communication Arts* or *Graphis Design Annual* for initial design inspiration. I did this not in search of a solution to a design problem I was facing, but in search of designs that, while unrelated to the project at hand, had something in common. That something was a design solution that was fresh, powerful, and relevant to that which it was representing.

Looking at page after page of world-class design is beneficial in two ways. First, one's standards are elevated by exposure to the best work being done internationally. Second, reviewing a few hundred outstanding designs, be they brochures, Web sites, or environmental graphics, usually results in a handful of stickies, marking pages to be revisited. Whether there's a motif, color palette, or image that jogs the creative

Designed by Jack Gernsheimer, the 1972 Boscov's logo, despite its shortcomings, endured for twenty-seven years. Two weaknesses of the original mark were the trendy, and thus non-enduring, nature of the *B*, and the fact that a noncompatible, preexisting script accompanied the original mark. Both of these issues were addressed when the logo was redesigned in 1999. As the designer of both marks, I feel the latter version shows a matured approach, and will not get dated, as did the first version, because the *B* is taken from customized yet minimally stylized script.

process, by the time the design it influences is complete, the design should have—and usually does have—little or no resemblance to the inspirational source.

FINDING IMAGERY IN UNEXPECTED PLACES

Let's say you're designing a logo for a new line of circular saw blades. While imagery on a power-tool accessories Web site is a viable source of information on the appearance of a circular saw blade, looking at seemingly unrelated items may provide both the reference you require and the door to a visual stream of consciousness that can lead the designer to a far more interesting place. For example, in pursuit of the circular saw icon you wish to develop, why not look for objects, directly or indirectly related, which have in common a circular shape, a serrated edge, or a metallic finish? With the plethora of icons saturating the visual environment, it becomes more and more challenging to develop designs that are truly distinctive and outstanding. Finding unexpected, albeit appropriate, imagery for reference and inspiration can be very helpful in developing a uniquely relevant logo design.

BEWARE THE NONINSPIRATIONAL SOURCE

On the subject of seeking inspiration, an amusing, albeit potentially catastrophic, situation arose several years ago as I was presenting logo designs to the CEO of a multinational corporation. I had reduced to three the number of designs to be presented in an effort to simplify the decision-making process.

The presentation was good spirited, and the selection process induced a full and constructive discussion about the merits and concerns about each of the three contenders. After a considerable period of time, the field of three was reduced to two. After that, more discourse about merits and drawbacks ensued. Finally, the CEO made his decision, and although it was my second choice, everyone agreed it was a worthy selection and that it would serve the company well for a long time to come.

Over the course of the meeting, which was some two hours long, it had begun to rain, and now that we were adjourning, the rain was falling heavily. The marketing director of the firm suggested we put the presentation boards in a plastic bag I'd used to protect the boards.

As I retrieved the three boards from the CEO and began

sliding them into the bag, he stopped me and asked to have a look at the bag, which had originally been sent to us from a service bureau and had their name and logo on it. Coincidentally, the first initial of the service bureau and that of the company were the same, and in both cases there was a sphere in the center. Other than that, the bag design and the painstakingly selected logo design were as different as night and day. So distinctive were the two designs that it had occurred to no one that their designs had anything in common. The CEO, however, whose strong suit was neither a keen eye for design detail nor a keen sense of diplomacy, was seriously taken aback and terminated the project then and there. He was convinced we

had stolen the design from the bag, and wanted nothing to do with it, or with either of the other two, even though they did not include the central sphere in question.

Fortunately, the story had a happy ending because after hiring first one and then a second studio to design the logo, the client was displeased with the work of both studios. As a result, they invited us back to review the earlier submissions, sans the originally offending mark. The final logo selected was the second one under consideration at the rainy-day meeting a year earlier. The moral of the story: Your design can be influenced subliminally, even by works that don't appeal to you. Moral number 2: Don't reuse bags with poor designs on them.

CHAPTER 04

PUTTING "PEN TO PAPER"

01   02   03   04   05   06   07   08   09   10

THIS IS THE MOMENT ALL SERIOUS LOGO DESIGNERS WAIT FOR. IT'S THE

OPPORTUNITY TO MEET THE CHALLENGE OF EXCELLENT LOGO DESIGN

HEAD ON, AND TO CREATE SOMETHING MEANINGFUL AND OF GREAT VALUE.

BEGINNING THE DESIGN PROCESS

Now that you've done the due diligence, taken time to absorb all the information you've painstakingly gathered, and digested all the inspirational examples you've admired, you're ready to begin the actual design process. Whether you choose to generate initial logo design sketches by putting down ideas digitally or conventionally is your call. The purist might shudder at the thought of going directly to the computer to start designing a symbol or word, but there are times when that approach is acceptable. For example, if the first idea requires repetitive elements, precise geometric shapes, or complex letterforms, or if it emanates directly from an existing font, working digitally to build your sketches might be well advised.

Generally speaking, however, beginning with a pencil or marker on paper may still be the best way to approach this early stage of exploration. Why? Because it's generally better to put down a number of early ideas than to labor over a single one at the outset. There will be time to delve deeply into the development of worthy design alternatives later in the process, but initially, exploring a broad range of ideas superficially makes sense. Once you've taken the time to rough out early possibilities, you can determine which ones appear to be worth pursuing in greater depth.

LOOK BEFORE YOU LEAP

Some names and letter combinations lend themselves to design more easily than others. This also applies to icons, which can be easier to develop if appropriate imagery presents itself quickly. If the design is mainly typographic, short names or words are usually easier to work with than long ones, and some letters work together better than others. The same is true if the name has two or more words and they are of nearly equal length. For example, the words "Book Club" will pair up more easily than the words "Pop Corporation."

The same is true of logos. There are some products or services that lend themselves to imagery, while others don't. Take, for example, a financial institution. It's very difficult to find imagery that immediately suggests finance. The dollar sign, one of the first things that comes to mind, is totally inappropriate because it's not international, it's a cliché, and

The objectives of (then) National Bank of Boyertown's 1972 logo were threefold: give the symbol a feeling of growth, local color, and stability. The stylized tulip, designed by Jack Gernsheimer, incorporated floral imagery prevalent in local culture on such items as hex signs hung on barns to ward off evil spirits. The cropping that created a square base gave the mark strength and stability, as well as an enduring contemporary style.

Though it may appear simple, this logo took months to design. That may be attributable in part to the inherent challenge of developing appropriate financial imagery and in part to my inexperience.

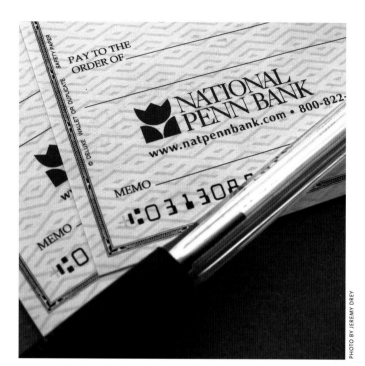

used in that context, it would be considered crass. It is also not unique or ownable, unless created distinctively in a style that negates these problems.

KEEP THE OUTER SHAPE IN MIND

As you initiate the logo design process, keep in mind that the outer shape of the mark will have a strong bearing on its overall appearance. Later, in the second section, you'll see that many of the classic logos have a basic polygonal or circular silhouette. Paul Rand's logo for ABC is a perfect circle, as is the outer shape of logos for GE, Westinghouse, Mercedes, International Paper, and many others. Ford and DuPont have had ellipse-shaped logos for a century. The Chrysler Corporation logo has a simple pentagonal silhouette. Bass Ale, Altana, and the Woolmark are triangular in shape, while Sun Microsystems and Dow Chemical have a diamond silhouette. Chase Bank sports a modified octagonal mark, while DSM, de Bijenkorf, and Entech Engineering are hexagonal. Swiss Air and the U.S. Postal Service are parallelograms. Square and rectangular logos include those for AIGA, Veer, National Geographic, H&R Block, and Levi's.

POSITIVE SHAPES AND NEGATIVE SPACE

Rather than feeling the compulsion to contain everything with hold lines, consider letting it bleed. Provided there is enough visual information to complete the picture, it can be very appealing to allow shapes to be defined without being completed. Among other things, interesting new positive and negative shapes and spaces emerge, which are intriguing in and of themselves. Give the viewer credit for having the ability to complete the picture. The effective use of positive and negative space can improve the balance and aesthetic appeal of the mark and can also accommodate additional relevant, albeit subtle, imagery.

In the case of the National Penn "tulip" (above), there is negative space that suggests a sense of growth. The solid base, a result of squarely cropping the leaves of the flower, gives the mark itself an added degree of strength and stability. This is desirable in the case of a symbol representing a financial institution, but might not be for a company distributing flower-related materials.

Whether or not negative-space imagery is introduced, the space itself must be handled thoughtfully. Clarity and balance can be compromised if the negative (or positive) areas within the mark aren't carefully considered. With the inclusion of negative-space imagery in the logo design comes the obligation to review the space when the logo is seen in reverse. On occasion, the negative-space imagery will not translate effectively and will thus be inappropriate or send the wrong message. This may require an additional logo for reverse treatments.

SHAPES AND SPACES MUST BE VERSATILE

Like positive shapes, negative-space imagery should be kept simple and be reducible without significant loss of detail, clarity, or recognition. If reduction compromises the inherent imagery, it compromises the entire symbol.

Ideally, a logo will not contain positive or negative areas that are very small. If negative areas are too small, they will tend to close up when the mark is reduced greatly. This can be a problem when the logo is printed, depending on the paper surface, line screen, or image quality. On a monitor, depending on its resolution and clarity, small areas within the mark can close up. If the resolution of the symbol itself is too coarse, it will compromise its appearance. As a rule of thumb, the logo should not have a resolution of less than seventy-two pixels per inch. The use of negative space to accommodate imagery can make the logo more special, but should not be done at the expense of legibility or reproductive versatility.

KEEP MARKS SELF-CONTAINED

Many people who attempt to design a logo feel the need to contain it in a shape, typically rectangular or circular. Most often, that shape is treated in outline fashion, so they end up with a mark contained within the outline of a square or radius-cornered box, circle, or oval. There are a few instances when this treatment works effectively, such as the original Northwest Airlines logo, in which the circular element serves as a compass and the arrow within the circle points to the northwest. This is justifiable because the circle is necessary to successfully communicate the visual and conceptual message. Regrettably, the 2003 redesign of the Northwest Airlines logo, while claiming to save significant cost on fleet painting, loses

much of the brilliance of the original mark (see page 129).

Another mark that uses a containing element appropriately is Paul Rand's logo, designed in 1962, for the American Broadcasting Company (see page 108). The symbol is comprised of a perfect outer circle, arguably the most enduring of all shapes, and contains three circular lowercase letters, which are strongly reminiscent of the Bauhaus font designed by Herbert Bayer at the Dessau Bauhaus in 1925. The lowercase letters are themselves comprised of nearly perfect circles, and arranged side by side, they give the mark a strong sense of balance and symmetry even though it's not strictly symmetrical.

More often than not, an outlined containment shape unnecessarily clutters and undermines the appearance of the symbol itself. One of the characteristics of a well-designed logo is self-containment. This means the mark holds together successfully without the need for devices that clutter and complicate the symbol. A rule of thumb in logo design says that if all things are equal, simplicity trumps complexity. The more clear and succinct the message, the more universally the logo will be understood. Additionally, the simpler the mark, the more successfully it will reproduce in varied sizes and media. All of these points suggest that if an additional self-containment element can be avoided, all the better.

BEGIN IN BLACK AND WHITE

Initial logo designs should be explored in black and white. Ultimately, the logo will have to work without the aid of color, but equally important, the designer can more effectively observe such things as balance, composition, positive and negative space, and general legibility if color is not yet introduced. Once the icon works effectively in black and white, color should only enhance it, provided it's sensibly introduced. Even if the logo is highly color dependent, like the WiTF logo on page 25, constructing and developing it in black and white first will allow the designer to look past issues of color and focus on more fundamental concerns.

Taking restraint a step further, eliminating even gray values makes sense because in its simplest form, the logo should work strictly with 100 percent black. Adding tones of gray is fine if you've addressed the worst-case scenario. What

This Charles Paul Jewelry logo alternative was designed in 2007. I allowed the script to bleed out of the box rather than contain it, resulting in secondary shapes that could be treated independently with slight color shifts. This expanded the palette and created a jewel-like appearance where subtle color variations lend a sparkle that one color often lacks. Care was taken to create smooth tangents at points where the letters bleed, giving the mark a more organic and pleasing look.

might that be? How about a want ad? Highly reduced size, poor paper (most likely newsprint), bad reproduction quality, and only pure black ink. If your logo design passes this test, you probably have a keeper. Here's where simplicity becomes desirable. When the mark is reduced to one-quarter inch, such things as intricate detail, thin rules, and small spaces will tend to reproduce poorly. As previously stated, a reduction version of the logo can be developed, but ideally, that shouldn't be necessary.

Finally, starting the initial client presentation with black-and-white designs has some real benefits. Most importantly, the client won't be distracted by this shade of green or the juxtaposition of tangerine and maroon. Once the initial options have been reviewed, showing the designs in color will make the alternative designs that much more appealing.

EXPLORING COLOR TREATMENTS

Once you've had the opportunity to develop and refine your design alternatives in black and white, introducing color into the equation is the next order of business. Color should never be treated as an afterthought, any more than the

selection of an appropriate font palette should be taken lightly. These are decisions that have a profound effect on the personality as well as the appearance of the logo. Ultimately, color will play a critical role in the success or failure of a newly designed mark. Just as limiting your initial exploratory palette to black and white is recommended, so is observing the logo in one flat color during this next design phase. As in the initial black-and-white studies, resist the urge to add blends and color combinations so that one-color options can be viewed as objectively as their black predecessors.

Once the single flat color treatments have been reviewed, select and test the color palette. In many cases, the designer will, in addition to selecting a default color, choose a number of compatible colors that can be used individually or collectively. These second-tier colors, along with the default color or colors, comprise the color palette. If the logo itself is multicolored, the various colors within it would become part of the palette. There may be instances when these colors are used independently. Let's say a Web site has five divisions, with a page or pages for each division. The Web designer may want to select five colors from the palette for the backgrounds. Perhaps a brochure

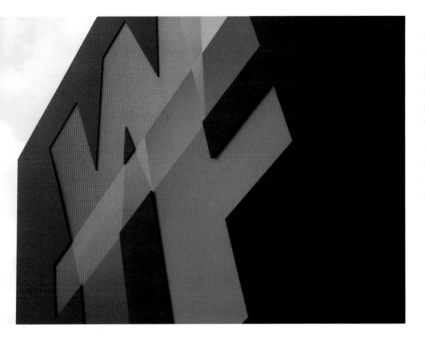

The logo for the central Pennsylvania multimedia group WiTF, designed in 2001 by Jack Gernsheimer, is a symbol sparkling with color activity. As the designer, I tried to avoid creating a symbol that was too color dependent, yet there's no question that this mark benefits dramatically from the vibrant gradients. The introduction of colors was done primarily to deformalize the media group. NPR affiliates can be perceived as stuffy, yet much of the programming isn't. Not only does the rich palette add sparkle and levity, it also suggests range and diversity, as TV, radio, magazines, and other media are divisions of this expansive company.

shows three product lines. Three colors from the palette can be used, each identified with one of the product lines.

While the default color should be used for the logo, a second or third color can be selected for use with the logo as well. From a branding standpoint, it's not recommended to use more than one color for the mark itself, as it tends to dilute the positive effects of consistent usage. It is acceptable, however, to use a neutral color like silver, black, or white for the mark. These options then become part of the first-tier color palette, while the compatible companion colors comprise the second-tier group, which are not used for the logo itself.

The selection of compatible colors is, in large part, subjective. Having said that, the designer has a responsibility to the client to select a color palette that reflects the personality and spirit of that which the logo represents. Just as inappropriate style or imagery is unacceptable, so also is an inappropriate color palette.

DON'T START WITH FOUR-COLOR EXPLORATION

Once the colors are selected, the designer should study the effectiveness of combinations of two or more colors. If the logo

is shown in color A, the logotype and tagline should be reviewed not only in color A, but alternatively in color B. In this way, the designer has the opportunity to determine which color combinations work together most effectively and which combinations should be avoided. On occasion, a color or value of a color will be selected in an effort to help prioritize information. For example, a mid-value color, which is of medium darkness, may be used for the larger logo or logotype, and a deep-value, or darker, color used for the smaller tagline. By doing this, the proper degree of emphasis on each element can be achieved. The same effect can be produced by using a color full strength in the smaller tagline and screened back to a percentage of the full value for the larger elements.

Once the black-and-white, one-color, and multicolor options have been studied, color blends and other treatments can be explored. If textural or painterly color is desired, now is the time to review those options. While it's tempting to offer the client a slew of colors to choose from, a somewhat restricted palette will simplify subsequent usage. No matter how many color options you offer, the default color should be used in most circumstances.

The ASPP logo was designed in 2000 by Jack Gernsheimer. I produced this mark during my self-proclaimed "Robert Indiana Period." Like the PACA mark (see page 22) and the WiTF symbol, the ASPP logo stacks two letters over two letters in a fashion reminiscent of Indiana's famous "LOVE" sculpture. That artist's signature image is the word "LOVE" in a two-letter-over-two-letter configuration, with the letter *O* distinctively tilted approximately forty-five degrees. The "LOVE" image was initially produced in 1964 for a Christmas card for New York City's Museum of Modern Art, and it was featured on a United States Postal Service postage stamp in 1973, the first in a series of "love stamps." "LOVE" sculptures stand in New York City and many other international locations.

BROADENING THE COLOR PALETTE

Second-tier colors can be helpful when a line of product groups or a number of divisions within a corporation need differentiation. One way of selecting a second-tier color palette is to place a selected color swatch directly beside the default color(s). Carefully observe the two colors side by side. The default color has already been established, so it's unlikely it will change. Therefore, if adjustment is necessary to improve compatibility, it will take place with the second-tier color. Once the default color and the first secondary color selection appear maximally compatible, you can select the next second-tier color and repeat the process. This time, however, you must strive for color compatibility with both established colors. With the selection of each additional second-tier color, compatibility with all the previously selected colors must be achieved.

The color selection process can take place digitally by building color swatches from CMYK, RGB, or the Pantone® swatch library. Colors can also be selected nondigitally by using the fan-type swatch books and holding colors up to one another and adjusting where necessary. A third way to choose a color palette is to collect colors from sources such as magazines, catalogs, fabric, and paint chips. Once collected, it will be necessary to scan the color or build it digitally.

GRADIENTS, BLENDS, AND OTHER COLOR TREATMENTS

The color palette does not have to consist merely of flat colors. The one established for WiTF is made up of a series of color gradients. In some cases, two gradients will have a mutual starting color and different terminating colors.

While call letters are almost always spelled out conventionally, this two-atop-two configuration consolidates and distinguishes the letters, while the overlap of top and bottom characters creates an additional cluster of resulting shapes. By stacking the letters, the overall mark becomes a square, making it tight, efficient, and easy to work with.

DEVELOP COLOR PALETTES FOR VARIED USES

As is the case with flat colors, there must be a strong sense of color compatibility across the entire palette when using colors incorporating blends or gradients. While blends may be treated as default colors, it's important to offer a simplified, nonblended version of the logo, as well as one-color and grayscale versions of the mark. Without these options, problems will arise when reproduction limitations are encountered. Note that the default palette is determined by the most common usage of the logo. In the case of WiTF, for instance, that is on the video monitor. For that reason, the default color blends are created in RGB and established for viewing with rear illumination. A print version of the blend must then be developed in CMYK, matching as closely as possible the appearance and intensity of the RGB, monitor-based version. This is not always an easy task, and some experimentation may be necessary in order to achieve a viable match.

Once colors have been selected, test printed, adjusted, and finally accepted, proper usage must be determined. This is typically discussed within the standards manual. Just because two colors share a common palette doesn't mean there won't be some restrictions. For example, chartreuse and tangerine are compatible colors, but placing tangerine type in a field of chartreuse is certainly not advised because legibility will be poor. It's impossible to create standards that cover every usage issue, but general usage standards should be established and good design sense applied when new treatments are explored. If desired, some or all of the new treatments can be included in the standards manual updates, which should take place periodically.

SOMETIMES IT'S EASY, OTHER TIMES IT'S NOT

As very young men, John Lennon and Paul McCartney would "come together" at one or the other's house and, with remarkable prolificacy, crank out songs over the course of a night's work. Very often, the next morning they would select those songs for which music had been written as the ones they ultimately produced, leaving those without music undeveloped never to be heard. One can only imagine the great works that found their way only to the trash can. One thing is certain: The lads often wrote works that simply flowed out of the pen but sometimes struggled to craft a song that the listener assumed was effortlessly created. They were undoubtedly aware that in many cases, to paraphrase their mates Ringo and George, "It don't come easy." The same applies to all forms of art: poetry,

prose, dance, drama, and many others. Logo design is no exception.

FIGHT THROUGH THE TOUGH TIMES

There will be times when ideas will start to roll out more quickly than you can put them down on paper, and times when you'll struggle mightily to eke out a few fledgling ideas. Why does this happen? Perhaps it has to do with your present mood; maybe it's your biorhythms; sometimes you have a mental block, a kind of brain freeze.

Just as there are struggles, there are times when obvious solutions present themselves like so many gift-wrapped presents waiting to be opened. By the same token, great design concepts can be as illusive as a championship in Philadelphia. When it's a struggle to begin designing, it may become necessary to jump-start the process. Said Pentagram's Michael Bierut of Paula Scher's Citi logo, designed in 1999: "Sometimes I'll work on a problem and one solution will come forward that has a rightness to it that just comes from sheer, stupid good luck. The Travelers logo was a red umbrella. . . . You put a red arc above [the *T* in Citi], and the result sort of accomplishes many things all at once, including symbolizing in some subtle way the merger [of CitiBank and Travelers]." (Fast Company.com, "Parsing Pentagram," January 1995, Steve Kroeter.)

LET THE PROCESS TAKE YOU

As a logo design unfolds, astute observation is of key importance. If a design is deemed worthy of development, hitch up your wagon and let it take you on a joyride. There are few experiences more exhilarating for a designer than watching a design emerge and come to life. It doesn't happen with each design you pursue; in fact, it happens rather rarely, but when it does, Katie, bar the door. It's as though a dramatic transformation suddenly takes place and a sense of life has infused itself into the design. That doesn't mean the design has necessarily arrived; it may in fact have a long way to go to completion. It does mean, however, that you're really on to something, and instead of pushing the design from iteration to iteration, you're suddenly being pulled through the refinement process with a dizzying force.

At first glance, the CCES symbol might be seen as a stylized eye or an abstract, symmetrical icon. When viewed in the context of a card, flyer, Web site, and the like, it takes on a more specific meaning. The logo, which I designed in 2005, utilizes two letters *C* symmetrically treated, representing arms lifting hand weights in a victorious, over-the-head position. Looking deeper into the icon, there is the discreet representation of breasts, as the majority of the cancer recovery clients are women recovering from breast cancer. At the same time, the somewhat abstract subtlety of the symbol does not exclude men and, in fact, could represent hand weights and pectoral muscles. The overall simplicity and shape of a rounded diamond, also used internally to represent the head of the subject, makes this mark self-contained and recognizable even after extreme reduction.

If you are working on the computer, in a program like Illustrator, stepping and repeating the design gives you the opportunity to save every step and to return to an earlier version if that's desirable. With each step, stand back and study the most recent version and determine what if any modifications are needed to improve it. While observing the effect of subtle changes, it's easy to lose sight of the big picture.

STEP BACK EVERY NOW AND THEN

To guard against losing sight of the big picture, and overlooking other possible paths in doing so, the designer should observe both the inherent details and the overall symbol. By doing that, subtle refinements can be made to improve the evolving mark while emerging imagery can open new exploratory paths. An open mind often allows the designer to observe and pursue directions not initially considered. When unanticipated gems present themselves to the open-minded designer, a new path opens up for tangential exploration. Whether that freezes the initial study or opens a second one is ultimately the designer's decision. The important thing to keep in mind is that the design process, if allowed to evolve and flourish naturally, often produces unexpected results that may well have potential qualities not inherent in the initial studies.

In the end, it may be tough to select only one variation of a design. In that case, select a few worthy variations on a theme and let the client be part of the editing process. Just be careful not to offer the client any design alternative that you wouldn't feel comfortable being the final selection, because if it's presented, it's fair game and might be chosen.

ESTABLISH MULTIPLE CONCEPTUAL LEVELS

Nothing adds to the depth and relevance of a logo more than a strong concept. Unfortunately, it's an element of logo design often overlooked. Creating a lyre out of the mirror-image S's in the Steinway & Sons logo gives it an added dimension, making it that much more intelligent, distinctive, relevant, and appealing. Even if the concept is subtly integrated into the design, it may eventually emerge and be recognized by the viewer. Some logo designers take the concept a step further and incorporate multiple levels of imagery into the mark. It's a little like leaving the flat chessboard and graduating to 3-D chess.

This deceivingly simple mark, designed in 2002 by Jack Gernsheimer, says a good deal more than one sees at first glance. The central figure is, by association with the name and context, that of a woman. Each of the initials, *W*, *I*, and *C*, in addition to standing for the organization's name, are used in the construction of the imagery.

The letter *W* suggests a shrugging of shoulders, and the use of modified serifs as hands reinforces the conveyed sense of the exasperation felt by a woman at her wit's end. This is the unfortunate lot for many women and children seeking refuge at the Berks County, Pennsylvania, shelter. The lowercase letter *i* serves as the body and head of the subject. Together, the letters create a figure that seems to be gesturing, "Where do I go and what do I do to get out of this intolerable situation?" The letter *C* suggests a sphere of protection provided to the visitor in her hour of need, which is the function of this benevolent organization.

The introduction of conceptual imagery, while desired, should not be done at the expense of the fundamental logo requirements. For example, if an incorporated image impairs the legibility or reproducibility of the mark, work should be done to correct or eliminate the problem area.

Appealing as supplemental imagery can be, it can sometimes become a liability. While literal images can add relevance to logos, an ambiguous symbol allows the company to venture into new sectors, if they choose, without having the logo imagery become inappropriate.

A CASE IN POINT

The Chicago Pharmaceutical logo, designed by John Massey in 1965, suggests a serpent that has the general shape of the caduceus, based on the Hermetic astrological principles of using the planets and stars to heal the sick. In recent times, the caduceus has become associated with the practice of medicine. Some medical organizations join the serpents of the caduceus with rungs to suggest a double helix. Massey executed this concept with simple elegance, uncompromisingly creating the letters *C* and *P* out of the serpent in a way that takes on the shape of the winged staff (see page 113). By doing this, there is an immediate association with medicine, and the letters themselves have a distinctively original and contemporary appearance.

Still other examples of subtly integrated imagery include Berks Women in Crisis and Certified Cancer Exercise Specialists.

The imagery in these logos is intentionally discreet and nonliteral because of the sensitivity of the subject matter it represents. Secondary and conceptual imagery can be subtle. It's not necessary to hit the viewer over the head with imagery that is immediately recognizable and obvious. In fact, it's often desirable to let things emerge and reveal themselves over time. If the mark works well on other levels, such as reproducibility and legibility, the multiple concept aspect can be a bonus— desirable but not essential.

01 02 03 04 05 06 07 08 09 10

WHILE THE LOGO IS THE HEART OF THE CORPORATE IDENTITY CAMPAIGN, IT'S

NOT ALWAYS AN ESSENTIAL ELEMENT. TYPOGRAPHIC TREATMENTS SOMETIMES

WORK AS WELL AS OR BETTER THAN A SYMBOL TO IDENTIFY AN ENTITY.

EXPLORE CUSTOMIZATION OF LOGOTYPE

The development of a logotype, the word that accompanies the logo or stands alone in place of a symbol, is a critically important part of the visual identity design process. If the name accompanies an icon, the selection of the font is based primarily on the need for compatibility between the two elements. Because there's some degree of subjectivity at play in the selection, it might be easier to employ the process of elimination, first determining font categories that are inappropriate. For example, from an aesthetic standpoint, if a logotype is going to accompany an airy logo, perhaps constructed of thin rules, it seems unlikely that a bold font such as Impact would be an appropriate choice to accompany the symbol. If elements within the logo run strictly vertical and/or horizontal, it makes little sense to introduce an italic or oblique word. If the mark has a very traditional quality, then a futuristic or even markedly contemporary font such as OCR would seem ill advised.

MAKING THE INITIAL FONT SELECTIONS

Physical characteristics inherent in the symbol aren't the only factors to be considered in the selection of the font that accompanies it. There are other considerations to be addressed, including style, theme, era, and those specific to the product or service. Once again, through the process of elimination, we would shy away from a thinly elegant cursive font for a line of farm tractor replacement parts. By the same token, a line of aromatherapeutic cosmetics for women would not be appropriately represented with its name set in Clarendon bold caps. By eliminating the obviously inappropriate font families, you will begin to see appropriate contenders emerge. Once that happens, it can be helpful to look at a font book that separates fonts into distinct families. Once you've narrowed the choice to a type of font—for example, a block serif—you can zero in on the contenders with the best feel. Should it be extended or condensed? Should it be italicized or Roman? Should it be all caps, cap initials, or lowercase? These are all relevant questions to consider as you strive for the perfect marriage of font and accompanying symbol.

VISUALLY STUDY THE LETTERS AND WORDS

Once you've zeroed in on the right category or subcategory of fonts, it can be helpful to type the word out in each of the

The New Man logo designed by Raymond Loewy is more a product of astute observation than of outstanding design. The treatment of the characters is similar to that of some of the letters in Herb Lubalin's Avant Garde Gothic. In the case of New Man, only the *N*'s read without problem. The *M* and *W* are not as quickly readable, while the *e* and *a* read rather poorly.

The logo for Taylor Security & Lock was designed in 2008 by Jack Gernsheimer. Initial exploration suggested that the three initials, *T*, *S*, and *L*, were difficult to work with and did not lend themselves to either symmetrical treatment or even comfortable balance. Deeper exploration revealed that an ambigram could be developed to add playfulness and visual appeal without significant loss of legibility. Like the New Man logo, this typographic cluster reads the same rightside up and upside down.

Enclosing the letters in a radius-cornered box helped to contain the mark and make it easier to work with. Additionally, the central letter *S* is held securely within the framing letters, reinforcing a sense of protection provided by the company's products.

The DesignWorks logo was designed in 1993 by Jack Gernsheimer. It represents an architectural firm that does a mix of commercial and residential design. The name is a play on words, and in that playful spirit, the words are run together without separating space. Instead, the two words are built in a serif and sans serif font. The type was set, and the weights and shapes were modified in an effort to achieve a high degree of compatibility. As the designer, I added an architect's scale to the edge of the business card. This was done because I had worked with the firm's principal to design my home months before. If I'd had access to an architect's scale when faxing ideas back and forth, it would have been very helpful because we'd both have been working at the same scale, making it easier to compare and update sketches. Equally important was the message and the enhanced visual appeal of the folding card.

selected fonts. Do this alternatively in all caps, lowercase, Roman, and italic. Some options will be obvious rejects and can be deleted immediately. As the viable candidates emerge, and there should only be a few, you can place them in the proximity of the symbol and observe how they feel together. You can also start the process of juxtaposing the two elements to get a sense of how the word and symbol best relate to one another. Should the mark be on the left, should it be on top, or should both options be observed? Should the symbol be large or small relative to the word? These decisions will need to be revisited, as will the final choice of font families, but for the sake of initial font selection, general "lockups" of font and symbol can be helpful, if preliminary.

While observing how the word looks in different fonts, sizes, and positions, the designer should also be scrutinizing the word or words to determine if there are things that can be done to improve legibility or to customize some or all of the letters and their relationships to one another. Often, a ligature can be created to improve the relationship of one character to the other. This should be considered if it facilitates the readability of the word. One of the virtues of a ligature is that it adds to the customized nature of the word. Beware, however, of creating undesirable ligatures. Too much of a good thing can undermine the appearance and readability of the logotype.

AFTER TEST FONTS ARE SELECTED

Once the preliminary selection process has been completed, it's very likely that modifications to some or all of the letters will result in a more distinctive, memorable, and visually interesting logotype.

Two examples of custom logotypes I've designed are Alan Behr (see page 86) and DesignWorks. The logotype designed for photojournalist Alan Behr, like that of DesignWorks, has the two words running together, separated not by a space but by a change in gray value. If "Alan" is a dark gray value, "Behr" will be lighter, and vice versa.

The letters are custom built, designed to be starkly simple yet have a contemporary flavor, and they will endure because of their simplicity. A basic grid was constructed, and each letter was drawn from that grid. The ascenders are intentionally short to keep the element sleek and low.

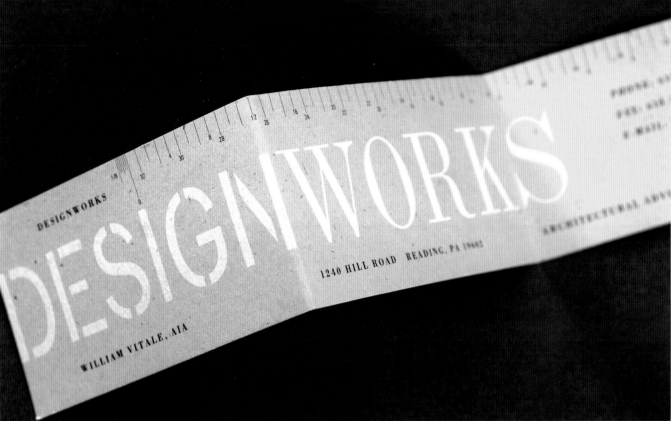

Logotype refinement is usually called for. Perhaps it's the rebuilding of an *O* into a perfect circle, or the height reduction of an ascender or descender, or the straightening of a line two degrees off true horizontal. The designer also makes decisions involving kerning. Should the letters be packed tightly, set at the prescribed spacing, or tracked out widely? Build, observe, and then select the best treatment.

Many times, a symbol replaces a letter in the logotype. If this is done effectively, it won't compromise legibility. Integrating the letter/symbol into the interior of the word is often done successfully, but replacing the first or last letter of the logotype with a symbol will usually impede legibility and is therefore not advised.

In some cases, this technique gives the appearance that the word starts on the second letter, or ends on the second-to-last letter, therefore causing the name to be misread or even read as another word. "Coat" can become "oat," "flight" can become "light," "plane" can become "plan," and sometimes the results can be downright embarrassing.

CREATING CUSTOM CHARACTERS AND WORDS

Creating a logotype from scratch or basing the letters loosely on existing characters can work very effectively if properly executed, ensuring a distinctly original logotype. Take a look at the work of John Langdon (*www.johnlangdon.net*), whose vision and skill in designing ambigrams—words that read forward, backward, and upside down—is nearly Escheresque in its brilliance. Admittedly, there is a compromise in the legibility of the words. This may or may not be acceptable in the case of logotypes, depending on the spirit of the client and the product or service being represented.

In the case of New Man cologne, the logotype is identical whether it's rightside up or upside down. While legibility may have been minimally compromised, it could be argued that the unique and appealing interplay of letters and words, and the resulting enhanced memorability and distinctiveness of the logotype, more than justifies this minor compromise. Besides, sometimes—though not often—clever for clever's sake is acceptable.

The Berks Packing logo, shown here stitched on a ballcap, was designed in 1991 by Jack and Jeff Gernsheimer. The meatpacking company was already well established in Berks County, Pennsylvania. As the designers, my brother Jeff and I decided that, because of the equity amassed, the existing script needed to be refreshed rather than abandoned. The new script, hand drawn by calligrapher James Lebbad, has far greater appetite appeal and typographic integrity than the old one (see page 56).

In the photo shown here, the leaping fish forms the letter *F*, the first letter of the name "Fisher." Among other things, one could argue that the word reads "isher." This treatment can be even more problematic when an otherwise strong design is compromised. This example illustrates the reduction in readability that often results from poor application of this technique.

REFRESHING OLD LOGOS

The 1972 logo for Boscov's was derived from a decorative font, designed by American typographer Ed Benguiat, named Charisma Script. The letter *B* was customized to bleed out of a circle. The sense of ingress and egress created by the very open mark invited the viewer to move through the mark in much the same way that the shopper is encouraged to meander through the aisles of the store. There is a casual and inviting sense about the symbol that is present in the stores, as well.

When asked to refresh the logo in 1999, we designed a custom script, which was then hand drawn by calligrapher Sherry Bringham. The *B* was taken from the name and integrated into the circle, thus ensuring total compatibility between logo and logotype. The bleed and circular shape borrowed from the predecessor strongly diminished the loss of equity garnered from the original mark, which was in use for twenty-seven years.

IMPROVE AS WELL AS REFRESH

When Berks Packing Company expressed a desire to grow their market geographically, my studio recommended

capitalizing on the equity of the general look and color palette they'd been using. At the same time, we advised taking advantage of the opportunity to design a new customized cursive word. The retention of the red and deep yellow colors helped the existing market recognize the brand, despite significant logo modification. Often, the viewer will not be keenly aware of a change in brand appearance if the change is not extreme, and little will be lost in updating the visual identity. On the plus side, a freshly reinterpreted identity program can revitalize and improve the look of the brand, generating new loyalty and an expanded market.

Along with a redesigned logo, new and improved package design can help increase sales. As new products spin off, they too will benefit from improved packaging and freshly designed advertising, point-of-purchase materials, and other applications.

Finally, the logo I designed for Blue Marsh Canteen in 1985 encircles a leaping fish with type, while the revised mark I designed in 2001 features a waterbird standing among the reeds and utilizes the reflection to create a sense of symmetry.

Another example of a refreshed logo is that of Reading Pretzel Machinery. The original version was designed in 1978, and it was refreshed in 1997. The redesign opportunity allowed me to refine the characters slightly and add a gradient to a previously monochromatic mark. The color blend added a level of relevance, introducing a suggestion of process and time, as the "dough baked," darkening as it moved through the oven.

The original Blue Marsh Canteen logo was designed in 1985 by Jack Gernsheimer. As the designer, I welcomed the opportunity to revisit the design in 2002.

The early mark arranged the name in a circular fashion somewhat suggestive of a life buoy. This treatment seemed appropriate given the restaurant's proximity to and shared name with a nearby lake. The leaping fish was not based on a specific type; rather, it was stylized and nonliteral.

Given the opportunity to redesign the mark seventeen years later, I retained the circular type configuration but changed the font. The positive waterbird was reflected in negative form. Along with the rippling water and grasses, the central area accommodated secondary and tertiary information, less essential than decorative.

The Boscov's *B*-in-a-circle logo, originally designed in 1972, was refreshed and updated in 1999 (see pages 38 and 39). At the time the earlier version was created, the department store chain consisted of four stores in the Reading, Pennsylvania, area. Today, Boscov's has fifty stores in six Mid-Atlantic states. Shown is a series of holiday shopping bags. Each holiday has its own color theme, and the drop shadow beneath the logo casts an appropriate image, such as a leaf on Thanksgiving, a shamrock on St. Patrick's Day, and a heart on Valentine's Day.

The Canal Street and Neversink Beer logos were developed in tandem, with the intention of giving the two entities a related yet distinctive appearance. Both marks were designed by Jack Gernsheimer in 1995.

The Canal Street Pub and Restaurant occupies a renovated factory building and is situated next to a canal that ran from Reading to Philadelphia. The barges were mule drawn, and the imagery shows the barge passing over an aqueduct. Liberties were taken to create an appealing scene where the smoke from the cabin stove reflects the shape of the river below.

The Neversink Beer logo, which adorned the amber bottles, shared a period style, color, and type palette with Canal Street. The initials *N* and *B* were good candidates for intertwining and gave the logo an established and cohesive feel. The addition of the grain and hops added embellishment and relevance to the mark. The resulting logo had the compatibility and period quality sought by the client.

The logo designed by Jack Gernsheimer for Showcase Station was also intended to evoke a feeling of nostalgia, in this case for the gas station of the first half of the last century. This venue for emerging musicians was a renovated gas station, offering ample opportunity for the introduction of wonderful genre imagery.

PERIOD- AND GENRE-SPECIFIC LOGOS

There are bound to be times in the career of a graphic designer when the logo design project calls for a mark with characteristics that make it specific to a period or genre. Broadly referred to as a "retro" mark, these marks are often both stylistically and thematically evocative of an era. When designing a mark of this kind, it's most helpful to research the look and feel of symbols from the time period. Notice how ribbons, containment shapes, multiple fonts, typographic manipulation, interweaving of elements, and other devices tend to flavor the mark.

In the case of period-specific logos, much of the information can be integrated into the symbol, rather than serve as detached accompaniment, as is often the case in more contemporary treatments. While many of the logo design rules can be broken when designing this kind of mark, characteristics like balance, typographic sensitivity, legibility, and cohesiveness are still worthy of retention. What may suffer is reducibility and simplicity, so one has to decide how much or little to deviate from the general objectives of good logo design. Shown here are a number of examples of this type of logo.

When called upon to design a logo from a specific genre, it's helpful to do due diligence and study existing symbols. Keeping in mind that there's a fine line between influence and plagiarism, one good idea can often spawn another. In the case of five logos I've designed that relate to Jewish organizations, the component they all have in common is the Star of David. Even though the six-pointed star seems an obvious choice and is prone to being cliché, there are always fresh ways of interpreting existing solutions. In this case, if one chooses to use the star, the challenge is to use it as a starting point and find novel and relevant ways to treat it. For example, the stylized pages of books are used to form the logo for the Holocaust Library, while various ethnic foods are used to build the Jewish Food Festival logo, resulting in starkly different results for two marks that utilize the same inherent image.

TOP: The logo for Reform Congregation Oheb Sholom, designed by Jack Gernsheimer in 1998, is a six-pointed Star of David, which has become internationally synonymous with all things Jewish. Because this mark represents a festival celebrating Jewish food, pictures of various ethnic dishes are used in each of the six diamonds that form the star. They include grapes (representing Manischewitz wine), kosher wurst or wieners, hamantaschen, whitefish, some ambiguous striped dish (perhaps sliced brisket), and, of course, lox and bagels.

BELOW, LEFT: The Reading JCC logo again utilizes the six-pointed star. In this case, a highly stylized letter *J* is repeated six times. Serendipitously, as the letter is turned sixty degrees, it can be read as a stylized *C*, thus reading as *JCC*. This is one of those happy accidents that happens on occasion. Most viewers might only see this once it's been pointed out. That said, the success of the mark is not at all dependent on that legibility because it's adequately distinctive to represent the organization effectively. This creates an exception to the legibility rule because the secondary imagery is subtly integrated and desirable, but not essential.

BELOW, CENTER: This logo, designed by Jack Gernsheimer in 1973, represents another interpretation of the Star of David. In this case, the basic element is a stylized human figure. When the six figures are rotating around a central point, they interweave, appearing to lock hands with one another. The figures form a bond of unity in which each individual is a critical link in the group, and they are vastly stronger together than apart. This logo was designed in response to the Yom Kippur War of 1973, and was a call for unity against attempted annihilation.

BELOW, RIGHT: The Sinai Academy logo was designed by Jack Gernsheimer in 2000 for a school focused on providing education with a Jewish perspective. Once again, the Star of David is utilized, this time as a central element rather than as the outer shape. Figures intertwine, raising the Torah over their heads in celebratory fashion. Each Torah is held by two people, imparting a sense of unity and representing a group of people with the common mission of providing and receiving specialized education. The conventional books not only fill out the logo visually but also represent the inclusion of general, non-Jewish studies.

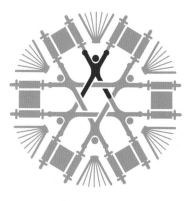

The logo for the Holocaust Library at Albright College in Reading, Pennsylvania, developed in 1995, consists of six groups of thirteen lines. Converging at ten-degree increments, they suggest an overhead view of pages in six opened books. Each "book" rotates sixty degrees, and the resulting negative space is the six-pointed Star of David.

Color plays an important role in this logo because the red converging "page" lines radiate a sense of intense heat while the black background in the negative star appears ominously morbid. The use of basic geometric shapes, the six-pointed star and the circle, ensures the classical nature and endurance of this mark.

01   02   03   04   05   **06**   07   08   09   10

GIVE YOURSELF AMPLE TIME TO PREPARE A COMPELLING PRESENTATION,

AND TRY TO AVOID THE "BOBBY! BOBBY! BOBBY!" SYNDROME.

"BOBBY! BOBBY! BOBBY!"

For those of you old enough to remember the movie *Broadcast News*, you're likely to recall a crisis moment when a local story was being fed to the network for live airing. Before breaking for a commercial, the anchor promised that when they returned, there would be coverage of the developing story. As the seconds ticked away, footage was to be sent, but a technical glitch prevented the feed from happening. As more time elapsed, a frantic local producer stood next to Bobby, the desperate technician. "C'mon Bobby!" she pleaded. "Bobby, c'mon Bobby!" "Bobby! Bobby! Bobby!"

I can't tell you how many times one of my studio associates or I stood by a churning printer, looking at our watches, chanting "Bobby! Bobby! Bobby!" Each time, we'd swear that would be the last time we'd allow it to happen. Of course, it's still the rule, not the exception. Proper time allocation can avoid Xanax® moments. If you pace yourself realistically, you can stay out of the angst-ridden crisis mode when it's time to head out to see the client.

EDIT AND SELECT ALTERNATIVES

Whether a studio full of designers or a solo practitioner is responsible for putting together the initial client presentation, many options should be considered preliminarily, but only those worthy of further exploration should be pursued. The client should be given the opportunity to review a range of viable logo designs that vary stylistically, conceptually, and iconographically.

If the logo being developed is a redesign or is meant to replace an existing symbol, at the very least, three alternatives should be shown. One alternative should be a variation somewhat similar to the existing logo. Perhaps this version is nothing more than a cleanup of the current symbol and logotype. The second variation can be a proposed design that varies dramatically from the existing logo. The third alternative should fall somewhere between the two extremes. By doing this, the designer gives the client the option of staying close to home and feeling comfortable on familiar ground, or venturing into new territory or even totally uncharted waters. The likelihood is that the more conservative the client's personality, the less adventurous he will be, probably going for the "safest" alternative. Conversely, the less conservative the client, the more inclined she'll be to take a risk and go for a significant departure from the existing logo.

TRY SEVERAL, PRESENT FEW

If the logo being designed is not replacing an existing mark, a variety of optional designs should be explored. In a fashion somewhat similar to that of the redesign approach, the client should be shown a number of alternative designs ranging from conservative to unorthodox.

After a good number of design alternatives have been conceived, examined, analyzed, nurtured, and taken down the path of evolving design, it's time to determine which designs are worthy of further development and which are doomed to the cutting-room floor. Most designers have a tendency to be parental about their creative efforts. The designer also wants her client to know he "got his money's worth" by showing all the hard work and precious time spent in arriving at this point, hoping all the invested effort will thereby add perceived value to the final product.

There can be a tendency to want to take many varied designs and prepare each for presentation. While that approach may be viable on occasion, it's not usually prescribed. There's something to be said for reducing the number of design alternatives presented to a more manageable, even very limited, number of choices. Keeping the selection process a clean and simple one is often desirable.

TOO MUCH OF A GOOD THING

When presented with too many alternatives from which to choose, a client can become overwhelmed with choices, thus making the selection process difficult and even unpleasant. It's perfectly OK to keep additional arrows in the quiver, or designs in your back pocket, as the case may be, in the event that the client doesn't gravitate naturally toward one or more of the presented alternatives. Rather than presenting everything at once, it's generally good to present only the top three to five alternatives out of the selection process. In fact, depending on how confident and competent the designer is, it may be desirable to show only one design, thereby taking the selection

component out of the client's hand and giving him the simple option of accepting or rejecting the single submission. Some designers feel that their authority and stature will be diminished by giving up the final logo design choice to anyone but themselves. When that is the case, it's the designer's responsibility to make that point clear and receive the client's consent at the outset.

MAKING A "SUICIDE" PRESENTATION

One clear advantage of presenting only one alternative is that it eliminates the distinct possibility that the alternative selected is not the best alternative presented. Of course, only those designs the designer recognizes as worthy of selection should be presented. That said, there's no guarantee that the designer's top choice will be the anointed one. Remember also that while the client may not have the training or skill needed to recognize a clear standout in a strong field, he has a greater understanding of the product or service, as well as the many aspects of the market to which the logo speaks.

Ultimately, understanding the client will help determine whether or not a "suicide" presentation is advised. Some clients would resent their exclusion from the selection process, while others would welcome it. Some truly enjoy being integrated into the entire process, while others may feel insecure about having the last say in a decision of such importance to their company. Understanding the level of involvement a client desires to have in the entire logo design process will help determine the best course of action regarding how many alternatives to include in the initial presentation.

ACTIVELY INVOLVING THE CLIENT IN THE PROCESS

Keep in mind that having a client figuratively looking over your shoulder can be either a good or a bad thing. If clients share similar aesthetic predilections, their involvement can be valuable. If they have a strong sense of style or if they have a love for the design process and don't want to miss out on what can be a rare and thrilling experience, they may make a number of positive contributions to the ultimate product.

I once worked on a project with a mother, father, and son literally sitting behind me as I worked on their logo. It was clear they were enjoying seeing their mark emerge and offered ongoing thoughts and suggestions on what was developing. Fortunately, they had a common vision coupled with good taste. As a result, the contributions they made to the design of their logo were positive, and the family felt a great deal of pride in and ownership of the final product.

If, on the other hand, the client lacks a strong aesthetic sense or has a tendency to head down an ill-advised path, there are likely to be problems and mutual frustration between the client and designer. Sometimes, four eyes are better than two; other times, the fewer eyes, the better. Understanding the pitfalls as well as the benefits of single versus multiple design submissions, and factoring in previously discussed variables, will help you make an informed decision.

REFINE AND SIMPLIFY

Once the finalists have been chosen and the rejects eliminated, it's a good idea to revisit the alternatives and do some cleanup and simplification of the soon-to-be-presented choices. This is a good time to step back and study the marks to see if and how they can be improved. Maybe you've already refined them to a point at which you feel they are presentable, but closer scrutiny can often suggest some alternative treatments that ultimately make the logo more successful.

Finding ways to simplify the mark, if that's possible, can prove beneficial once it is implemented. Not only does simplification facilitate adaptation of the mark to a broad range of applications, it also helps make it more memorable. Which of the following pairs of logos do you more readily recall: Chevrolet or Chrysler; IBM or Xerox; Betty Crocker or Pillsbury; CBS or NBC; the Gap or Banana Republic? I rest my case.

Unless you have an obscenely large number of alternative designs, it's a good idea to archive even the developmental designs that weren't selected for presentation, if for no other reason than to look back in years to come and observe the development of your designs. As an art student at Syracuse, I was advised to save all my sketchbooks. I pass that advice on to you and suggest also that developmental digital files be saved. Another reason for holding on to digital files is that on

occasion, you may be working on a project for which an exhumed design is nearly appropriate, in which case you can retrieve the file and resume the development process. Keeping notebooks with reduced printouts will provide quick reference and easy access to the desired files.

MEETING FACE-TO-FACE

Years ago, almost all presentations were given directly. On rare occasions, boards would be prepared and shipped off to a waiting client for review. Doing this could reduce the time and expense of the logo design project, but there were pitfalls. For one, there's no one there to introduce the presentation and go into detail about the marks to be presented. There's not likely to be the kind of dialogue that takes place when the designer or account executive is present making the presentation. This problem can be minimized by discussing the submissions by phone or e-mail prior to the presentation or conference calling during the presentation. Still, there's no assurance this will work as effectively as a face-to-face meeting.

A few years ago, I e-mailed a long-distance client with detailed notes regarding aspects of the preliminary logo presentation files that were attached. I cautioned that in this early stage, I was showing an illustrative style and that the content would change. The available horse illustration I used as a placeholder would be replaced with a dog if the idea flew. When the client replied that this service was for dogs and cats, not horses, I knew I was in trouble. Unfortunately, she failed to read the cover letter, and I can only imagine the discussion that ensued when the horse illustration appeared. Once things turn negative, as they did here, the rest of the presentation is tainted. By the same token, when things start out well, they usually continue to go well.

THE ORDER IN WHICH TO PRESENT ALTERNATIVES

About thirty-five years ago, I prepared a package design presentation for a very intimidating CEO. As we flew to L.A., Chris (the presenter) and I labored over the order in which we'd show the fifteen design alternatives. We decided to simply present them in the order of our preference, with the strongest first and the weakest last. When Chris began the meeting with some introductory information, the CEO snapped his fingers, rudely requesting that we cut to the chase and show the designs. Chris gingerly handed over the first board. After what seemed like an hour, the CEO, who was surrounded by his four henchmen, looked over at me and inquired, "You designed this?" "Yes," I said, my voice shaking. At the time I had a beard and long hair, and I'd heard the CEO was not a fan of the hippie movement. Another pause. "I like it," he said, at which time the four yes-men piped up with their sound approval. After that, every design, even the weakest, was praised. Of course, had the first comment been negative, the choir would have surely sung with many a sour note.

Today, it's common not to make the presentation to the client face-to-face, and boards with the various design options are no longer part of the process. That said, there's no substitute for a face-to-face meeting with the client. Of course, in today's digital world, our studio in Pennsylvania designed a corporate identity program for a manufacturer in Sydney, making that desired face-to-face presentation nearly impossible. In place of mounted boards, you're likely to attach a multipage PDF to an e-mail so your distant client can print out the pages and/or forward the file to other decision makers.

PRESENTING DESIGNS IN THEIR BEST LIGHT

Whether the first presentation is made at an actual meeting or a virtual one, how the page is displayed will have a bearing on how well it's received. Although there's no substitute for good design options, they will look that much better if they are well presented. Should they be formatted for printout on a tabloid (11" x 17"), U.S. letter (8.5" x 11"), A4 (8.26" x 11.69"), or a less-common size? It's a good idea to find out this information before proceeding.

To begin with, create a typographically appealing information area that will accommodate such information as presentation date, design round, client name, project name, and alternative number or letter. This gives you the opportunity to show off your typography skills, as well as to enhance the appearance of the presentation page.

Next, determine how you want the first view of the logo to appear. If in doubt, keep it clean and simple. Showing the logo

design by itself on a page, with plenty of breathing room around it, is a very good way to introduce each option. If you have a few variations on a theme, you can reduce them and place them on the bottom of the page. Understand, however, that if you do that, the secondary variations will likely be overlooked or thought of as inferior because of their subordinate placement.

SHOW MARKS IN HYPOTHETICAL CONTEXTS

No matter which way the designs are first viewed, the look of the presentation board will have a positive or negative effect on the outcome of the decision-making process. There are any number of ways to design the page, but they should have this much in common: First, show the logo sitting independently with plenty of "air" around it. Second, show the logo applied in one or more appealing hypothetical applications. This is an opportunity to place the mark in an enticing context, and it can even generate additional work if the client embraces one or more of the suggested applications.

Showing the logo on a polo shirt not only adds appeal to the mark, it also forces a good designer to confirm that the alternative designs are versatile enough to be reproduced in restrictive processes such as embroidery. Other hypothetical adaptations to be considered are business cards, a Web page, a vehicle, or environmental graphics such as a reception area. The idea is to keep the boards consistent from alternative to alternative and to make each option look as enticing as possible. At the same time, be certain that a hypothetical design is seen as preliminary. You don't want to spend lots of time designing a business card that, when the actual adaptation process takes place, is incompatible with other items.

TAKE A HOLISTIC APPROACH

The full adaptation process should be approached holistically, so for the initial presentation, make it clear that the applications are hypothetical and likely to change. They should look good enough to help sell the logo but not be so time-consuming that you waste money on an eventual throwaway application.

Once you've decided which contextual applications you

want to use (and you don't need more than two or three), find the imagery you need and build the application. You can treat everything as vector illustrations or find images to be used, though only for the limited purpose of making a small presentation. If for some reason the presentation images are used beyond this narrow scope, you'll have to get permission to use the photo and pay the usage fee, if necessary.

How the boards are laid out will either enhance or detract from the presentation. Of course, you want them to enhance, so design a pleasing page, and remember, the logo is the star.

DO PRELIMINARY LOCKUPS

When presenting logo designs to the client for the first time, the mark should, at a minimum, be shown with and without accompanying type. For one thing, it will assuage the fears of the decision maker who must select the final logo. Seeing the newly proposed logo design sitting by itself affords an unadorned or encumbered mark that can more easily be scrutinized and judged against the other options. It can also look detached, "naked," and even vulnerable with no accompanying type. Showing the logo alternatively with identifying type will reduce concerns by the client that people won't know what or who the mark represents. It will also give a better sense of how the symbol will be seen on most occasions—that is, accompanied by relevant information.

In order to show the logo effectively married with type, some exploration, albeit preliminary, must take place. Ideally, this should enhance the mark yet not appear etched in stone. It should be made clear that the type treatment shown in this first presentation may or may not change, as full exploration hasn't yet taken place. Keep in mind that you run the risk of having the initial type treatment requested by the client, so some care should be taken to show the accompanying type in a good light.

01	02	03	04	05	06	07	08	09	10

THE CHANCE TO MAKE A POSITIVE FIRST IMPRESSION ONLY COMES ONCE.

WHAT YOU'RE ABOUT TO PRESENT CAN MAKE OR BREAK THE PROJECT.

PREPARE CLIENTS FOR WHAT LIES AHEAD

Just as you might describe one friend of yours to another when introducing them, it's good practice to take some time to describe your logo designs to your client before unveiling the alternatives.

For the client, seeing the new logo for the first time is, to some extent, like first laying eyes on your newborn child. You know this is a person who will be a very important part of your life moving forward, yet she's a stranger starting out. You're aware that in time you'll be warmed by the sight of her, but today she's a newcomer, and a period of adjustment, albeit brief, may be necessary. Drawing this analogy for your client can help put him in the right mindset for the "introduction" to follow.

CAUTION: BEWARE OF PRECONCEPTIONS

It's a good idea to offer one other cautionary note: Beware of preconceptions. Most likely, clients will have some idea or sense of what their new logo should look like. It's inevitable that what you're about to show them will not match their expectations. It may in fact be far better than their preconception, but it will definitely be, to some degree, different. Try to assure your clients that this will likely take place upon first glance and that the inevitable discrepancy between what they expect to see and what they actually see ought not taint their first impression. Recognizing that, and truly keeping an open mind, will minimize any initial feelings of disappointment or displeasure.

While you have the option of saying, "Here they are," and laying all the alternatives on the table, most designers will prefer some conversation to start the meeting. It can be helpful to offer a brief description of what you're about to show. You might also want to go into a little detail about your initial thought process and how you arrived at the solutions you're about to present. You may in fact want to use the newborn analogy to prepare your client for a period of adjustment.

DESCRIBE THE QUALITIES OF A GOOD LOGO

Now that you've primed the pump, it's a good idea to reiterate the qualities inherent in a well-designed logo. By doing this, you establish a standard by which to compare the design alternatives you're about to present. This is information you may have discussed with your client previously, so an abridged version will suffice here. Now's the time to remind your client that a well-designed logo should be *attractive, cohesive, conceptual, distinctive, enduring, legible, memorable, relevant, sophisticated,* and *versatile.*

An attractive logo has visual appeal to the greatest number of viewers possible. A cohesive logo holds together, even when there are many components. A conceptual logo implies a sense of intelligence and creative flair. A distinctive logo has a unique appearance, distinguishing it from other logos. An enduring logo is timeless and will look as good in thirty years as it did the day it was designed. A legible logo reads easily and quickly. A memorable logo is easily recalled and recognized. A relevant logo uses imagery that pertains to the product, service, process, or entity it represents. A sophisticated logo exhibits a sense of good taste and decorum by avoiding inappropriate imagery, fonts, colors, and motifs. Finally, a versatile logo is reproducible in a wide variety of sizes, materials, and media.

READ YOUR AUDIENCE

Any presenter faces the challenge of continually assessing the situation. How much or little detail the introduction requires should be, to some extent, "played by ear." You will need to read your audience, whether it is one person or a dozen. If you get the sense that people are eager to have a look but patient, a moderately long introduction, perhaps two or three minutes, should be fine. If there's a lot of anticipatory squirming and a sense of impatience or annoyance, it may be time to cut to the chase. The same holds true as you're presenting the design alternatives to your client. Should you go into detail on every logo design before moving to the next, or should you keep the verbal description brief and encourage further discussion once all the options are on the table? Sensitivity to the mood of the group will help determine the pace and depth of your presentation.

There will be times when the client immediately gravitates toward one of the design alternatives and recognizes that this is without a doubt the winner. While that scenario is a desirable one, it's not always going to happen. You may even sense a bit of disappointment or ambivalence when the designs are first revealed, which is why the newborn analogy can help ease any anxiety the client may be experiencing. Try not to become distracted or tentative if this seems to be the case. Different people react differently, and someone who appears displeased may in fact be delighted by what he sees, and vice versa. It's fair to say that, provided the logos you're presenting are well designed, a winner should emerge from the pack and, as with the newborn, soon be embraced and appreciated for the rest of its life.

BUILD SUSPENSE

During the typical initial design presentation, there's a good deal of excitement about having a first look at something as important as a new logo. Imagine how exciting it is to buy your first new automobile. There's the initial research, followed by visits to showrooms and test drives, and then the final decision and the purchase of the car. In fact, the car will probably be with you for five years or so, and then the process will repeat itself, with diminished excitement likely following each purchase. A new logo, on the other hand, should be serving you for a much longer period of time—hopefully, four or five times the car's lifespan. One could argue that the logo selection decision, therefore, is five times as important as that of the car purchase. Whether or not that's the case, there's no denying that this presentation is a significant event for both the presenter and the presentee. As a result, there should be a high degree of importance placed on the selection experience. With that comes an opportunity to create a level of suspense prior to the first look at the designs. By taking advantage of that opportunity, the presenter can help increase the air of excitement and, in doing so, give the proper sense of significance to the upcoming experience.

A good presenter, like a seasoned fisherman, knows not only how to catch the fish but also how to bring it in. He knows just when and how to set the hook, and he has an innate sense of how much slack to give and when to take it away. Whether you're a natural when it comes to playing the audience or someone who doesn't possess that skill, you should try to take advantage of this rare opportunity to set the perfect table for the important upcoming event.

VIEW THE ALTERNATIVES

At long last, after all the exhaustive research, interviews, familiarization, pencil sketches, digital design exploration, development, refinement, selection, presentation, preparation, and final touch-ups, it's time to lay your cards on the table. Finally, after all the time and effort you've invested on behalf of this project, you have the opportunity to display the fruits of your labor, to present those designs you've been so diligently pursuing. The moment your client has been waiting for with bated breath since the project's introductory meeting has arrived, and the designs are placed or projected for initial review.

Once all the designs have been presented, either one at a time or all together, encourage discussion in which the characteristics and merits of the logo alternatives are considered. In each case, pros and cons should be aired; the options should be weighed on their own merit and also compared to the other designs under consideration. After the necessary dialogue, in which appropriate parties have had the opportunity to offer their thoughts and opinions, it's time to begin the process of elimination.

SELLING YOUR DESIGN

As a logo designer, you can expect a degree of reluctance on the part of the client. At some point in the process, they're likely to get cold feet and need reassurance that replacing their tired but familiar old friend with this new and unfamiliar upstart is the right thing to do. And once the mark is introduced, be prepared to face a cadre of naysayers who are convinced the old logo "ain't broke." In time, assuming the symbol is well designed, all but a handful of those resisting will learn to love that which they once resisted. Want to test it out? Save the business card of a reluctant client and wait two years. Now, show her the old card and ask if she'd rather go back to using the former card. Nine times out of ten she'll be amazed at how much better her new card looks, and scoff at the suggestion.

BEWARE THE NAYSAYER

Often, one or two people offer their opinion freely and in a committed fashion while others are reluctant to speak up. For that reason, some people can wield disproportionate influence. If the vocal minority add constructively to the discussion, no problem. If, however, they seem to be undermining the process and denigrating good alternatives, you may have to reclaim the floor and do some damage control.

The first designs selected for removal can be easy to choose. While all submissions must be worthy contenders, tighter scrutiny may reveal that some alternatives are stronger overall than others. Having eliminated the first options, begin the task of helping the client make the more difficult choice of embracing one of the remaining designs. Earlier observations can be recalled, and pros and cons weighed once more. This alternative is stronger in some respects than the others. Ultimately, a final decision must be made.

In some cases, the client will want to see some additional exploration done on more than one alternative. Any more than two finalists can prove problematic and costly to the designer, since the designer will be charged with producing a second round of design alternatives.

Now that an initial decision is made, there's typically a sense of relief felt by those who have been given authority to make the final selection. Nevertheless, there's usually more than a little enthusiasm expressed by all parties, and the next order of business is to move forward to finalize the chosen logo designs, making sure they will hold up to most if not all of the objectives defined at the onset of the project.

WHAT ABOUT COMBINATIONS?

The client should gradually gravitate toward one logo design, allowing the designer to move forward and refine the chosen mark. Of course, while desired, that's not always the case. In the worst case, the client may be displeased by all the submissions and terminate the job then and there. If, however, serious thought and good work has been done to produce the initial designs, it's highly unlikely that this scenario will take place.

What can and often does happen is that the client asks the

designer to take this from alternative *A* and that from alternative *D* and combine them into an amalgamated second-round alternative. In the spirit of cooperation, it's best not to offhandedly dismiss this kind of request. There may in fact be some merit in what is being proposed. If, on the other hand, you can clearly see that this attempted combination will not yield a favorable result, it's time to put on your diplomatic hat and explain to the client why you anticipate that this idea is likely to fail. This can be challenging, particularly for young designers who may understandably be intimidated by a CEO or other authority figure. If there's a reasonable chance that the combined mark could have merit, agree to have a look to determine the viability of the idea. In the end, it's important to be cooperative yet appropriately confident and assertive, knowing that it's in everyone's best interest to deliver an outstanding end product.

DISCUSS OBJECTIVES FOR THE SECOND PRESENTATION

To conclude the initial presentation meeting, briefly discuss once more what will be done between now and the next meeting. It's best to take detailed notes during the session and go over them together with the client before departing to be sure you're in agreement about what comes next. If possible, a second person can accompany the presenter and be the note taker. While you don't want to give the impression that you're ganging up on the client, an additional design representative can also be helpful in offering support and another advised point of view, if requested. Additionally, the two of you can discuss the meeting on the way back to the studio to confirm that you both came away with the same impressions and expectations.

It's a good idea to type out the notes as soon as possible after the conclusion of the meeting, while things are fresh in your mind. Send copies to all involved parties, clearly enumerating what must be done in the second design round. This is usually very much appreciated by the client, and it serves to underscore that everyone has the same expectations moving forward. It also reassures the client that you're serious and well organized.

Finally, agree on a date to reconvene. Depending on schedules and the amount of work to be done, you may choose to see one another within a few days or several weeks.

The idea to use sunglasses in the Look South identity program came quickly. It seemed appropriate to incorporate them directly into the name, replacing the letters *o* and *o*. Creating four cards, each with its own set of sunglasses, matched the playful personality of the Atlanta-based photo archive owner. The photos were lit so the colors of the lenses would spill toward the bottom right—or the southeast. The program was designed by Jack Gernsheimer in 2000.

Anna Fey

President

Look South, LLC

Anna Fey

President

300 Has

Look South, LLC

Fx: 404.8

Anna Fey

President

Anna Fey

President

Look South, LLC

300 Hascall Rd. NW, Atlanta GA 30309

ph: 404.874.4242

Fx: 404.874.4230 / eFx: 530.364.7277

annafey@mindspring.com

01   02   03   04   05   06   07   08   09   10

WHILE THE FIRST PRESENTATION IS ARGUABLY THE MOST IMPORTANT,

SUBSEQUENT ONES ARE CRITICAL IN SHAPING THE FINAL PRODUCT.

INITIATE SECOND-ROUND REFINEMENTS

You've now arrived at the point in the logo design process where you can focus your energy on one or two alternatives embraced by the client. The time you spend in this stage of the operation is typically very constructive. Often, there's a fair amount of wheel-spinning in the earlier stages. If you are not careful, you can blow the budget early on, tweaking alternatives that won't appeal to the client and are likely not to make the first cut. Also, keep in mind that if ten designs are submitted and only one is selected, 90 percent of your time and effort has no extended benefit to the client, yet it eats into your profits. That's not to say you should explore only two or three alternatives, but keep practicality in mind when determining how many ideas to pursue.

Now that the client has expressed her interest in one or two marks, the time you spend finessing the second-round design(s), particularly if there's only one alternative to complete, is time going directly into the development of the final logo. But before leaping into the second-round design, take a little time to observe the work that's been done to this point, including the rejects. We have a tendency to get so engrossed in the minutiae that we can't see the forest for the trees.

STEP BACK EVERY NOW AND THEN

While it's a wonderful feeling when you're in a "zone," where you are totally swept into the design process, it's easy to lose sight of the bigger picture. Stepping back and taking a fresh look at the work that's been done up to this point can be very useful. For one thing, you can get an overview to reset your sights; for another, you may see something you've pursued earlier that can strengthen the second-round candidate(s).

Keep in mind that the logo(s) you're now charged with refining have been selected by your client. Unless you've discussed specific changes, straying too far from the approved design could be problematic. It's easy to stray from the mark during the refinement process and come back with a design that is too radically changed. In order to avoid this, at least copy and paste the developmental steps so you can explain the evolution and return to an earlier iteration of the design, if necessary. This is good practice at any stage of the logo design process unless the design is too memory intensive. If a watercolor artist goes beyond the optimum conclusion point of a painting, there's little to be done to rectify the situation. If a logo designer has gone too far but has saved earlier steps, there's no problem.

INCORPORATE NEW OBJECTIVES

As you begin the second-round refinement stage, review once again the meeting notes you gathered at the original presentation. Get together with any associates who joined you at the meeting, and be sure you have a clear sense of the objectives for the second wave of development.

It's important to remember that the client has expressed an interest in seeing further development, if requested, of only the selected design(s). At the same time, by keeping an open mind, you may stumble across an idea that really excites you. If that's the case, you might find a way to integrate that idea into the selected logo you're refining, showing it as an alternative, a variation on a theme. If that compromises the original alternative, you can develop the new idea and show it to your client, expressing your enthusiasm for this emerging candidate. Keep in mind that you run a small risk of upsetting the client by straying from the approved logo. For that reason, you need to have a sense of whether or not the client will be receptive to a new alternative at this stage in the game and act accordingly. From a budgetary standpoint, the less time you spend developing this new alternative, the better. If it's embraced, you'll have the opportunity to do all the refinements needed to finalize the mark.

Just because you've reached this stage doesn't mean ideas will stop emerging. What you do with the ideas is your call. Even if you decide it's too risky to show them now, you may want to put them in an idea file for use in a future project. As your career expands, you might amass a sizeable collection of rejects and undeveloped ideas that can be recycled for presentation somewhere down the line. Odd as that may sound, many rejected logo designs have been exhumed and embraced when later chosen for an appropriate purpose. For an example, see the story about the "reincarnated logo" on page 39 of chapter 3.

REFINING THE LOGOTYPE

By now, you've given initial thought to the selection of fonts that may become part of your new visual identity program, and the client has had a first look at the type that directly accompanies the logo. You may or may not want to reexplore the many options open to you. While your initial exploration into logotype alternatives has been completed, you should now be reviewing your choices and deciding whether or not the fonts you first presented are ideal or if other candidates should be considered. Now that the symbol has been selected, you can feel free to spend more time reviewing other possible logotype options, knowing the time won't be spent in vain.

The large number of fonts readily available today is a double-edged sword. If you are discriminating, as you should be, you'll have the opportunity to consider hundreds of viable options, but if you don't effectively employ the process of elimination, it's easy to become overwhelmed by the myriad possibilities.

SELECT FONTS THAT SUIT THE COMPANY, MISSION, OR PRODUCT

The personality of the company or product line you're designing for will have a significant bearing not only on the flavor of the logo but also on that of the accompanying fonts. And now that the logo has been approved, you may want to delve more deeply into the font selection process than you did initially.

The first thing to consider is the logotype itself. In addition to the selection of a thematically appropriate font to start the process, it's important to observe the way the letters within the name interact. This can have a significant influence on the font selection, letterspacing, creation of ligatures, and general arrangement. Take, for example, the word "minimum." All those *m*'s, *n*'s, and *u*'s are begging to be tightly kerned in a customized lowercase condensed Bauhaus-like font. On the other hand, a word with lots of *a*'s, *o*'s, *c*'s, and *e*'s might be telling you to consider Futura Light lowercase and to play with the circular elements at your disposal. An example of that can be found in the logo for the Picture Archive Council of America, known as PACA, on page 79.

EXPLORE LOCKUPS

Now that the logotype has been finalized, determining how it relates to the logo—assuming there is one—is the next order of business. In general, it's good to have three optional "lockups"—that is, fixed relationships between the logo and the logotype. Ideally, there should be a lockup that fits well in a relatively square area. There should be one for a horizontal space and one for a vertical space, as well. The most expendable of these is the vertical option. Having format options will allow the logo cluster—any combination of the symbol, name, or tagline—to fit in a variety of areas. This is particularly helpful when there is limited space to accommodate the cluster. For example, if the cluster is relatively square and the available space at the bottom of an ad or within a banner ad is very horizontal, the resulting consequence is a small cluster and small components, which may create legibility or reproduction problems. If, on the other hand, a horizontal lockup is provided, the components will have greater size and presence.

SIZE AND DISTANCE RELATIONSHIPS

An important part of the lockup design process is determining the size of the elements and the distances between them, and positioning them in relationship to one another. If the logo within the horizontal lockup is placed to the left of the logotype, as it often is, its distance from the beginning of the logotype must be established. It's most convenient to have a measuring device inherent in the logotype so that measurements will be based on an existing element rather than on conventional units of measure such as inches or millimeters. Selecting a letter from within the logotype to serve as a unit of measure ensures that it will be present whenever it is needed and that the distances will be consistent whether the logo is enlarged or reduced.

Typically, the height of the selected character is used, and a letter with a flat top and base, such as an *E*, is chosen. Using a letter with a rounded base is not advised because it is more prone to misreading, while the characters with flat bases and tops provide a precise measurement. Prior to the selection of a measurement character, the distance to be determined, such as the distance between the logo and the logotype, should be established optically. Once the space has been determined

There are five acceptable configurations of type and logo in the PACA standards manual. Alternative 1 allows the logo to be used independent of type. Alternative 2 arranges the type in a justified stack with the word "Member" on top of the stack. Alternative 3 is the same as alternative 2, without "Member." Alternative 4 has the acronym centered above the logo and the name centered beneath. Alternative 5 has all components on one line. These acceptable configurations ensure that the logo and name will fit well in the available space, be it horizontal, vertical, or square.

In the example shown, the height of the letter *E* in the name Carpenter serves as the basic unit of measure, and its height is called "1 *E*." If half units are required, the height of the *E* is reduced to 50 percent, and that unit is called "½ *E*." These units are then used to determine the area of isolation and other measurements of importance.

CARPENTER
Specialty Alloys

CARPENTER

based on what looks and feels appropriate, the measuring unit can be selected and, if necessary, modified.

ESTABLISHING THE FONT PALETTE

Once the logotype and its relationship to the logo and tagline has been nailed down, it's time to finalize the choice of accompanying fonts. Arguably, the most important criterion for font selection is aesthetic compatibility with the logotype and/ or symbol. Font availability is also important. Default fonts such as Times are always good candidates because they have a classical quality that keeps them from looking dated. In addition, they have a neutrality that makes them broadly compatible with logotypes, which are often not neutral. Times is highly legible, so large quantities of text can be read quickly and easily. Also, the Times family is large and includes a number of weights, as well as true, not obliqued, italics. In addition to compatibility and legibility, fonts loaded into Word are nearly universal in their availability, so they can usually be used worldwide by designers, printers, Web developers, and others who are working with the new identity program.

Other serifed font families, such as ITC Century, are

excellent choices because in addition to a variety of styles and weights, there are condensed alternatives that are sometimes welcomed. Because it's commonly believed that when it comes to reading large quantities of text, serif fonts read better than sans serif, the font palette should include at least one serif font family. It may also be helpful to include a sans serif family in the font palette, and variety within the family, such as a condensed version of the font, can prove helpful as the identity program is adapted for future applications. Once again, neutrality, availability, versatility, and classical endurance should factor into the sans serif font family selection.

BUILDING THE COLOR PALETTE

As was the case with fonts, a final color palette must now be established. In selecting a group of colors for the new identity system, the colors chosen should first and foremost be chromatically compatible. If Pantone® 032 red is the main color, chances are that other richly saturated colors will work best when the red needs to be accompanied by secondary colors. If, on the other hand, smoky pastels make up the palette, a bright turquoise is an unlikely choice as the principal color in the new system.

If, as should be the case, the designer has already established that the mark works in black and white, the next color-related decision should be the principal or "default" color of the logo and logotype. The logo needs to work in one color, and the selection of that color is critically important because it will have a strong influence on the perception of the brand. Imagine the classic Coca-Cola script in lavender, or Paul Rand's eight-bar IBM logo in chartreuse.

SELECT COLORS THAT FIT THE COMPANY WELL

The personality of the company or other entity being represented by the logo should be reflected in the main color choice. The secondary colors, if needed, should reinforce the primary color. For example, a logical main color for an aquatic-related company is aquamarine. One could make the argument that the color has been overused for product or corporate identity and has become cliché. If that is cause for concern, a less likely color can be chosen, provided it isn't obviously inappropriate.

What are examples of inappropriate color? How about chrome yellow for a psychologist's identity, seafoam green for a line of heavy construction equipment, or lavender for a line of chainsaws? Again, one should remember that the principal color must have enough strength to stand alone as a one-color logo, and it should be dark enough so a tagline can be read off of a white background without difficulty.

Colors in the palette should have CMYK, RGB, and Pantone® or other spot-color equivalents. If gradients are inherent in the palette, they should list the start, middle (if necessary), and end numbers. Other information, such as drop-shadow coordinates, should be included in the standards manual or style sheet so they will be faithfully reproduced by anyone working with the logo, whether it is a sign manufacturer in Tokyo or a print shop in Topeka.

THE SECOND PRESENTATION

The second logo presentation, perhaps less dramatic and exciting than the first, is of nearly equal importance. No matter how much or little the refined logo differs from the originally presented mark, the clients will be eagerly waiting to see what is likely to be the final appearance of their all-important new logo. Since the logo is of such significance to the branding process, the anticipation and level of expectation can be very high. While it's less likely to happen in the second round, there may still be a discrepancy between the client's preconceptions and what is presented. If the initial presentation produced one or two clear and strong contenders, it's highly likely the refined version will meet with only a heightened level of approval. If, on the other hand, the first round of designs missed the mark, the second round must be on target if there's any chance of winning back a level of confidence and enthusiasm.

It's a good idea to enumerate the points that were raised in the original presentation prior to introducing the new design(s) so the client has a clear recollection of discussion points that have been addressed.

MAKE A BIG THING OF IT

While the drumroll fanfare that took place at the first presentation may not be necessary, the design soon to be revealed is also very important. This sense can and should be heightened by a spirited prelude to the unveiling. A good presenter knows how to "play" that energy appropriately. Rehearsing this is a good idea for young designers, knowing that in time it will become easier and more natural.

Once the final designs have been presented, discussion should be encouraged. Even more than in the first presentation, hybrid solutions should now be avoided, if possible. If a request for a color or font change is made, chances are the resulting change won't significantly compromise the mark. Try to avoid making additional changes that undermine the strength of the icon if you know it will result in a weakened logo. The more you base your reservations on objective points, the better. For example, if asked to integrate a circle where a star should be, you might say that the star creates a more distinctive and balanced negative space, while reinforcing the fact that the telescopes the symbol represents facilitate stargazing.

If the second presentation is successful, you should be able to walk away with a clear winning logo that is, if not complete and ready to adapt, very close and in need of only minor revision, which can be approved via PDF review within a day or two.

CHAPTER 09

AFTER THE FINAL SELECTION

01 02 03 04 05 06 07 08 09 10

ALL THE GROUNDWORK HAS BEEN LAID. HEADING INTO THE HOME STRETCH,

THE TIME HAS COME TO DOT THE *i*'S AND CROSS THE *t*'S.

SEEK CLEARANCE OF THE MARK

Before venturing into the development of final art, it's a good idea to consult a trademark attorney who can search the design mark to make sure it is not too close in appearance to another mark. There are companies who specialize in searching for uses of a name or design throughout the country using the U.S. trademark registry, state trademark registries, business names, and Internet searches. If the mark will be used internationally, you should consult an attorney regarding nondomestic searches. Companies can register marks either in their state, if the use is local, or nationally with the U.S. Patent and Trademark Office, if the use is interstate. The trademark examiner assigned to the application will also review the mark and may reject it if there is a conflict with another logo in a similar business sector. The general rule of thumb is that if no similar mark is being used by a similar business, there will be no confusion or conflict between two logos, and your symbol will be approved and granted trademark status. This means that you have priority over the mark in your industry.

BE SURE IT'S AN ORIGINAL

If it's been determined that the logo is too similar to another and could be confused or associated with another entity within the geographic area or the sector in which the mark is used, the mark will not be able to be used. That's a tough pill to swallow after all the work that's gone into the development of the logo. It's tougher, however, if much additional work has been done to create final art, and much worse still if a good deal of money has been spent to print business cards, stationery, and related materials. It gets even more costly if environmental graphics such as exterior and interior building signage have been produced and installed.

Because of the proliferation of symbols floating around in the ether, there's a possibility that your newly designed logo might inadvertently be too similar to an existing mark and thus cause potential confusion in the marketplace. For that reason, your client should contact an attorney who specializes in trademarks to be sure the symbol will clear. Once clearance has been confirmed, you're free to move ahead with the development of finished art of the logo and other components of the identity program.

PREPARE "FINAL ART"

At long last, the selection and clearance process is complete, and it's now time to develop final art for the logo. This may involve nothing more than renaming the design to indicate that it is complete, but there will likely be lots of details to attend to. Depending on the complexity of the design, this can be a short or lengthy process. If there are a number of layers in the design, it will be best to flatten them when all is complete. It's important, however, to save a preflattened working file of the final selected mark so you can, if necessary, return to an earlier stage and extract or change something. It's best for the designer to hold onto the preflattened file to avoid any confusion regarding which is final art. Giving prefinal files to the client can increase the risk that the improper file will be used.

If there are masked elements within the logo, it's good to turn them into clean, unmasked components so that the logo will be easier to work with and accidental unmasking will be impossible. Zooming in on the logo in outline rather than preview mode will allow you to check that things are true horizontal and vertical and that any inherent angles are correct. Elements should all be checked for alignment, and final adjustments should be made. If the final version has text within it, it should be converted to outline, so fonts need not accompany the logo when it's distributed.

CONVERT FROM CMYK TO RGB TO PANTONE®

Typically, the EPS (encapsulated PostScript) files are saved with all colors created out of cyan, magenta, yellow, and black (CMYK). This file format is used when four-color process printing, sometimes referred to as full-color printing, is being done. In addition to CMYK EPS files, other EPS files are saved with the logo in one default Pantone® color or two or more Pantone® colors, depending on what is needed. The TIFF, JPEG, GIF, and/or other bitmap-type files should be saved in the RGB color mode, since they will be seen on a monitor, not in print.

CMYK files should be used for anything that will be printed in full color (four-color process), either by your personal computer printer or by a professional print shop. TIFF files supplied in this color mode can be imported into Microsoft Word documents. One-color black files are the logo configurations in their 100 percent black color mode. These could be used for faxing, photocopying, or other black-and-white printed media. The print Pantone® files contain the two-color version of the logo configurations, which should be used for business cards, letterheads, envelopes, or anything that will be printed in just those two colors.

PREPARE FILES IN VARIOUS FORMATS

To use the new digital logo art fully across all media, you'll need to prepare it in a broad range of file formats. The number of formats you provide depends largely on the way the logo will be used and the budget. At the very least, the logo should be saved in one vector and one bitmapped file format. That way, the client can take responsibility for having the logo saved in additional formats, if needed. An Adobe Illustrator EPS file can be provided to anyone who will be printing the logo.

If there is more than one lockup, it will be necessary to save each one in every file format being prepared. The clients should be informed that they need to back up and store the original files in an appropriate and accessible place and distribute copies to those who need them. It's not the designer's responsibility, unless contracted as such, to continually provide copies of the logo to the client. Every time a file is retrieved, it takes time to find and send it, and typically no one wants to absorb the cost for the time spent.

Web RGB files are not intended for printing and should only be used for on-screen use, such as in e-mail or on the Web. These are compressed JPEG files, optimized for screen viewing. If printed, they will not look clean and sharp, particularly if they are dimensionally large in size. The descriptions below will be helpful in determining the correct file format to use for various applications.

- ENCAPSULATED POSTSCRIPT (EPS): This file format is the desired one for use when the logo is being printed. Because it is a vector file, it can be enlarged or reduced with no deterioration of image quality. It can be problematic if a user takes liberties and modifies aspects of the mark. For that reason, it's important to establish and adhere to standards to preserve the integrity of the mark.

- **Portable Document Format (PDF):** This graphic file is also used widely by printers. This file format will also preserve the vector graphics. It was created and is controlled by Adobe Systems, which is both PC- and Mac-compatible.
- **Tagged Image File Format (TIFF):** This type of file does not preserve the vector graphics or any editing capabilities. These files are most commonly used in a program like Microsoft Word. A photo-editing program must be used to make changes to a TIFF file.
- **Joint Photographic Experts Group (JPEG):** This is a compressed file that should only be used on screen, in e-mail, or on the Web. JPEG images will not print with crisp edges. A photo-editing program must be used to make changes to a JPEG file.

THE BRANDING CAMPAIGN STARTS WITH THE BUSINESS CARD

The logo should be seen and used as the cornerstone of the branding campaign. At this point, decisions need to be made regarding the extent of adaptation. Ideally, the designer can take a holistic look at the branding campaign and, along with the client and marketing strategist, decide where and how the new logo will be applied.

A good way to start is by designing the business card. For one thing, nearly everyone who has a new logo will need to have new business cards on which to place it. While the business card is not necessarily the worst-case scenario, its small size, coupled with the amount of information to be prioritized and accommodated, presents challenges. The lockups of the logotype to the logo will need to be finalized in order to design the business card. In addition to color, typographic issues can now be addressed. Fonts, point sizes, kerning, leading, arrangement, relationship, and prioritization of information all must be considered.

TAKE TIME TO SELECT THE RIGHT PAPER

Early decisions to be made include whether the card is one- or two-sided, whether the card is flat or folded, and how many colors will be printed. Paper stock is also a serious consideration because it will affect the entire stationery package. Be sure that the stock you specify is still available. Papers come and go, and the swatchbooks provided to design studios are often not replaced until after they are rendered obsolete. Also, be sure that the paper you recommend has envelopes, text, and cover-weight stocks necessary to flesh out the program. Paper color and surface are also important considerations. Does off-white or lightly colored paper feel appropriate, or is white a better choice? If so, how bright should the white be? These decisions have a bearing on how the printed image will appear. While a bright white, coated surface will generally give the brightest and truest color, an uncoated off-white stock may be a better candidate if the tactile qualities of a softer, less-bright sheet prove a more appropriate selection. My studio once produced an award-winning catalog on uncoated paper that was printed to appear the color of light buckskin. At a dinner celebrating the receipt of the design award, the printer's rep said to the company president, "If you think that looks good, you should see it on a coated stock." No sooner were the words uttered than a hush fell over the group. After a flustered explanation was offered, nothing more was said. The next catalog, however, was printed on a bright white, coated stock and was not nearly as well received in the field, showing that the trade-off between image quality and tactile sensation should be seriously considered.

THE NATURE OF THE COMPANY INFLUENCES THE CARD'S DESIGN

The nature of the company, the impression one wants to make, and the budget will determine how elaborate the business card should be. Sometimes, understatement is called for; other times, extravagance is appropriate. Die cutting, embossing, and foil stamping are all possibilities, but restraint is often the best approach.

If the business card is two-sided, the information-intensive side can be done in one color and the more visually interesting side in four-color. The options are many, and this is the time to explore the color palette and its various treatments. I recently designed a business card with the information and logotype presented in black and white on uncoated stock. The reverse

This logotype, designed in 2006, was commissioned by a New York–based photographer and journalist. Because of the brevity and balance of the name, it seemed workable to run the two words together and separate them by a shift in value. The letters were constructed using a very simple grid. The short ascenders are one-third taller than the other letters, and the width and height of the lowercase characters, with the exception of the letter *l*, are equal. The rounded corners and ends deformalize the type, and the spirit of the letters is contemporary, with predictable longevity, thanks again to the distilled simplicity of the shapes.

Despite the distinctive appearance of the characters, the compromise in legibility is minimal.

The business card for Alan Behr was designed in 2005 by Jack Gernsheimer. I felt it was important to select a stock that matched the personality of the client. I sensed that beneath the veneer of this straightlaced New York intellectual property lawyer there lurked a photographer and writer with conviction and passion. I chose to support the idea of extreme contrast by specifying a duplex paper that had a soft matte finish on the side with type, and a deeply rich red high-gloss surface on the other.

PHOTO BY TERESA VAN WAGNER

alanbehr

side of the card was simply high-gloss red using duplex stock. The understatement of the information side was counterbalanced by the rich color and finish of the other side. This felt appropriate because it matched the personality of the photojournalist, whose cool exterior contrasted with a passion seen in his photographs.

DESIGN ENVELOPE ALTERNATIVES

Using the business card as a reference point, you now have the tools you need to adapt the logo to other items in the stationery package. At the very least, you'll want to provide your client with a letterhead and envelope. American letterheads are almost always 8.5" x 11"; corresponding envelopes are 4.125" x 9" and are known as #10 envelopes. While it's a great design project to "push the envelope" while designing it, it's rarely advised. Having a color or pattern printed on the inside requires printing, die cutting, and converting the envelope. This may be justified if the envelope plays an important role in the visual identity program. There are typically minimum quantities required in order to convert envelopes.

A return address is usually printed on the face of the envelope, and it usually resides in the upper left-hand corner. Occasionally, the return address is placed elsewhere on the face, but care must be taken to ensure that the design complies with postal regulations. If in doubt, check with the U.S. Postal Service at *www.usps.com*.

TREAT THE ENVELOPE LIKE A COMPOSITION

Return addresses are sometimes placed on the flap of the envelope, which can have a pointed or flat base. When adapting the logo to the envelope, consideration should be given to the mailing address. Will it be handwritten or printed? If printed, will it be direct or on a label? If it's on a label, will the label be transparent, translucent, or opaque? Other elements that must be considered are bar codes, indicia, or postage stamps. The stamp will be cancelled, adding to activity in the upper quarter of the face. There may be bar codes at the bottom, as well, and they need to be added to the mix. When all the components are in play, you can create a composition that has all parts relating properly to one another. Now you can address whether the logo is included, and if so, how prominently. Think of the design on the envelope as a composition of parts that are properly prioritized and relate aesthetically to one another.

DESIGN LETTERHEAD ALTERNATIVES

As mentioned, the standard American letterhead is 8.5" wide and 11" high. Though not essential, the vast majority of letterheads will be this size. Now that two pieces of the stationery program are in place, designing the letterhead should take cues from the previously designed pieces. In most cases, it's desirable to concentrate the activity in the upper quarter of the page, leaving ample room for the body of the letter. The inside address, greeting, and salutation are all part of the mix and should be properly placed relative to the body.

Because you're dealing for the first time with a substantial amount of real estate, you can be more generous in the space, given the components. Typically, the logo will remain locked up with the logotype. You might want to experiment with a repetitive pattern, an enlarged logo that contrasts minimally with the paper color, an embossed or hot-stamped logo, or other less-conventional treatments. The important thing is to design appropriately for the client. A soft hot-stamped logo that may work perfectly for one is obviously inappropriate representing another.

COMPOSE THE LETTERHEAD WITH FUNCTION AND FORM IN MIND

The letterhead design offers an opportunity to show off the logo in its best light. Like the envelope, the design of the letterhead should be approached as one would a painting, with all parts properly prioritized and relating to one another in a balanced and pleasing fashion.

Covering the page with ink, and even fully printing the page to make it appear another color, can work effectively. You can then reverse out of that color for certain elements, such as a large logo. This treatment can also be considered for the back of the sheet, offering exciting possibilities upon folding, where color meets color.

It's important to keep practicality in mind and be sure all information is legible. If faxing or photocopying is necessary, only a very light color will work properly. Die cutting, special folding, and other novel treatments should be considered, but only if the end result works well within the new identity system and imparts the appropriate message about the entity that is being represented.

DESIGN ADS

Another ideal opportunity to test, adjust, and develop a full branding campaign is designing a series of ads incorporating the new logo and motif. It's important to keep in mind that, while the logo should have a shelf life of twenty or more years, the look of the ads will change much more frequently. This allows the designer the opportunity to be more experimental. In turn, the various advertising design approaches will start to reveal what works and doesn't work within the campaign. For example, if, on a small black-and-white ad, sunrays in a logo compromise the clarity, then they may need to be modified or eliminated. The more the logo is worked with, the more familiar the designer will become with the strengths and weaknesses of the branding identity. Given the opportunity to resolve issues at an early stage can really help get the bugs out of the campaign. At the same time, a series of ad templates can be created and used for subsequent ads, either by the brand-identity design team or by an internal or freelance designer.

DESIGN ENVIRONMENTAL GRAPHICS

No application of the logo is more dramatic, exciting, and gratifying for all involved than the design and production of environmental graphics. Generally consisting of interior and exterior signage, environmental graphics might also include the use of graphics as part of the décor. Be it subtly applied to a wall behind the receptionist or on a sixty-foot-high oil tank, adaptation of the new logo to environmental applications can be a relatively inexpensive way to showcase the new identity system.

When it comes to directional signage, clear communication is first and foremost. Working hand in hand with a proven sign manufacturer can save time and money down the road. Be sure that the designs you propose are producible and affordable, or give a range of alternatives of varying expense.

The curved wall behind the receptionist's desk at the new office facility of C. H. Briggs Hardware served as an excellent backdrop to accommodate the logo, which Jack Gernsheimer redesigned in 1998. The standoff letters utilized a subtle tonal shift to separate "CH" from "BRIGGS" without the need for space between the words. The wall and truck applications offer opportunities to introduce a dramatic sense of scale to a corporate identity program.

C.H.Briggs Hardware Co., Inc.

CHBRIGGS

Distribution. Marketing. Solutions.

From banners to door pulls to carpet patterns, properly integrating the new logo into the spaces where people work, eat, walk, and congregate will help to involve people in the new campaign. By doing so, they will be likely to embrace the new program more quickly and fully. Because of the permanent nature of the application, care should be taken not to overdo the integration of the logo. If kept appropriately subtle, it will endure more successfully than if it's too "in your face." If contrast is important, as in the case of directional signage, that must be addressed. Otherwise, understatement is generally advised.

If the logo is to be applied to clothing such as golf shirts, it may be necessary to design a simplified version for embroidery. Consulting with specialists on apparel decoration is advised.

DESIGN WEB, TV, AND INTERACTIVE GRAPHICS

The Web is an increasingly important application for the new logo. It will almost assuredly be seen on both the home page and the back pages. A good logo will even reduce to fit on the left-hand side of the URL field. If there are thin lines or spaces, it may be necessary to modify them for this use. Another consideration is logo animation. Designing a

storyboard, or at least giving thought to possibilities, will be helpful in the event animation is desired.

Designing a Web or TV version of the logo, if you choose, offers you the opportunity to capitalize on the ever-expanding capabilities of dynamic media. Here's a chance to add color and light activity, dimension, motion, and other features not available in conventional media. Although currently common, it's perfectly acceptable and sometimes desirable to deviate from the default symbol when using the logo within dynamic media such as the Web site. Keep in mind that this is still part of an overall branding system. Consequently, there must be adequate continuity and similarity to inform the viewer that the modified logo is a recognizable part of a larger visual identity program.

Typically, the Web-oriented logo should be saved in JPEG or GIF formats. The JPEG is a light file and handles many colors well. The GIF is even lighter and may be desirable if there are a limited number of colors. I've discussed file formats—including Web-appropriate formats—earlier in the chapter. A potential pitfall to avoid is creating a symbol that slows down the Web experience. People have very little tolerance for lack of speed when they are online.

UTION. MARKETING. SOLUTIONS.

RIGGS

GS.COM

01   02   03   04   05   06   07   08   09   **10**

GREAT EFFORT HAS GONE INTO THE ESTABLISHMENT OF A CORPORATE IDENTITY

SYSTEM. NOW IS NOT THE TIME TO CUT CORNERS.

PRESERVING YOUR INVESTMENT

Few things have the potential to deteriorate faster than a corporate identity program, especially a logo that is used incorrectly. The best way to ensure proper usage is to establish a comprehensive standards manual. The style guide, as it is often called, doesn't need to be overly extensive or terribly costly, but it needs to clearly explain how to use the logo in various applications. The manual can't cover all usage questions, nor should it, but it needs to address issues that commonly need clarification.

To begin with, it's most helpful to include a letter from the CEO or a person with equivalent clout. If that person explains the importance of adhering to the identity system, it both validates the program and emphasizes its importance to the overall branding mission. A good logo is designed to work hard for decades, and anything less diminishes the investment made in its development.

Once the general importance of the campaign is discussed, follow by offering a brief explanation of the logo, including any symbol's inherent message and other points of interest. This

information can be accompanied by an image of the basic logo, and possibly also by the logotype.

LOGO CONSTRUCTION AND AREAS OF ISOLATION

When introducing the logo in the standards manual, it's good to familiarize the viewer with the inner workings of the mark. Showing the logo in a dissected form will give all who work with it a deeper sense of understanding and appreciation for the symbol. Very often, significant time and effort goes into the nuances that make a mark special. Why not share that information with those who will be charged with treating the logo faithfully? If it's apparent that the designer has gone above and beyond the call of duty to create a special mark, those who work with it will be more inclined to show the logo the respect it deserves, rather than treat it with casual disregard.

Next, areas of isolation can be discussed and illustrated. This will familiarize the viewer with the amount of space desired to allow the logo to breathe and avoid unwanted encroachment with the mark itself. There may be exceptions to

Shown here is a layered view detailing the construction of the logo for the Berks County Community Foundation (see page 152). The mark consists of four diamonds clustered together to form an overall diamond shape. A sunburst radiates from the center of the cluster. Various yellow, blue, and orange gradients color the logo.

Additionally, information on the construction of the Carpenter Technology Corporation logo can be seen on page 80. By showing construction details in the standards manual, the logo's handler has a better understanding of the composition, as well as the proper appearance of the mark. With this knowledge, there's less likelihood of incorrect alteration or unadvised usage.

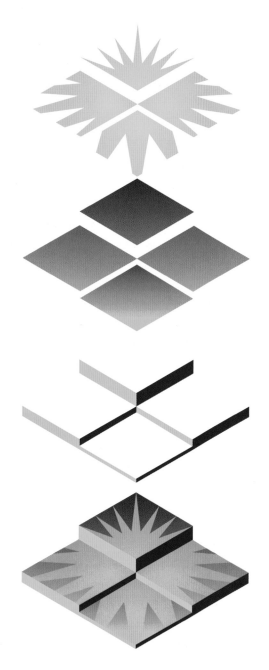

the area-of-isolation rule that should be discussed, such as supergraphic treatment. In some cases, the logo may become an independent graphic rather than a corporate identity element. For example, if the logo is used dramatically on a wall in the conference room with minimal contrast, you may want to run type or other images over it. Making an exception to the area-of-isolation rule can allow for this and other creative treatments of the mark.

LOGO/LOGOTYPE RELATIONSHIPS AND COLOR ISSUES

The standards manual should discuss "lockups" of the logo, logotype, tagline, or other key elements. As mentioned earlier, time and care should have been put into the important development of relationships among these elements, and a minimum of two or three lockups should be offered. This will allow the groupings to fit into relatively square, horizontal, and extreme horizontal spaces.

After lockups are presented, font and color palette issues should also be discussed. Included in the color area should be a detailed breakdown of color gradients, CMYK and RGB builds, as well as spot colors. A good example of this is the WiTF logo, which can be seen on page 25.

Also included in this part of the standards manual should be a show of the various fonts selected and a brief discussion of proper usage. In an effort to preserve the integrity of the program, noncompliant colors and fonts should not be introduced into the system.

RETAIN THE FONT AND COLOR POLICE

I recently provided a client with a reprinted standards sheet, along with the disk of alternative logo files and formats. The client's company had just launched a new Web site, and upon visiting it, I noticed the logo was displayed on the home page with total disregard for the accompanying typography. After painstakingly developing a system of lockups for the logo and logotype, it was frustrating to see blatant misuse of the system. In this case, receiving another standards sheet and disk gives the client a chance to treat the elements properly. In doing so, as I informed the client, the client's employees will preserve the integrity of the system and see it used properly. If they choose to ignore it, they've essentially thrown their money away, because nothing erodes a corporate identity campaign more quickly than allowing everyone who touches it an opportunity to reinterpret it. In surprisingly short order, there will be inconsistency and insensitivity undermining even the finest design.

Next, show a business card and letterhead with labels indicating placement and specifications of all elements. Fonts with sizes, tracking, leading, and any other characteristics should be shown. Color treatments should be labeled, as well. In some cases, it's helpful to include a final page or two on logo usage "dos and don'ts." While all violations can't be covered, the most prevalent ones can.

SOMETHING THE CLIENT CAN HOLD ONTO

Once the standards manual is complete and ready to turn over to the client, give it some added value. Design a cover and spine for the loose-leaf binder or simple folder that holds the manual. Print and insert the cover and spine into the acetate sleeves. Select a binder that has at least one inside pocket so that additional items can be accommodated. When you think about it, there are few tangible items initially generated in a corporate identity campaign. That will change as stationery, signage, and a slew of other applications are produced. For now, the binder gives the client something to have in hand. Adding stick-on pockets to accommodate CDs is advised, as is printing nicely designed labels for the disk.

A lot of blood, sweat, and tears have gone into the development of the new identity program. The more professional the package you present, the greater its perceived value.

KEEP IT FLUID

When providing the client with the standards manual, discuss the need to keep the standards document fluid for one year's time. This will allow the client to become familiar with the system and will allow the designer to make additions, deletions, and changes where necessary. Is an extreme horizontal lockup desirable? Should a two-color version be added? Is further explanation necessary for clearer communication?

Actual application of the identity program can reveal aspects that can be improved upon in ways not visible before the program is put into practice. Ideally, the logo's designer should be given the opportunity to implement any changes. If that's not the case, he should serve as a paid consultant.

When working with their new logo, the good folks at the Image Works found that a number of suppliers offered to "clean up the broken-up image," assuming that the logo was meant to be solid rather than broken up. An addition was made to the standards sheet explaining that it was intended to be broken as shown because it represents a stamped image rather than a clean, mechanical one. Situations like these suggest that changes may well occur, and modifications to the program, and consequently to the standards, are to be expected.

IN CONCLUSION

With every passing year, our visual environment becomes more and more saturated. Centuries ago, that meant new vegetation, additional shelters, and a proliferation of species. In today's world, it means an ever-increasing bombardment of imagery, much of it produced to generate increased revenues. We encounter promotional imagery in the form of ads in newspapers and magazines, and on Web sites and TV. We see billboards and signs in retail environments and on vehicles—pretty much everywhere you look. The objective of most promotional campaigns is to raise brand awareness. Well-developed corporate identity programs facilitate this ongoing effort. Dig deeper, and the nucleus of corporate identity is the logo.

Whether for altruistic nonprofit groups or corporate entities, good logos work very hard to properly represent the organizations they symbolize. Designing those logos is an exercise in editing, refining, and distilling information into a concise and precise element. When done well, the logo has great value, which grows over the years as it stays in the public eye. With time and exposure comes familiarity, which often generates trust. Trust, in turn, helps the buyer or beholder feel a higher level of comfort when interacting with the company, their products and services, and even their personnel.

The longer a logo endures, the greater its value. As we've observed, there seem to be certain qualities in many of the

Shown below is the D & D Technology business card. Please adhere strictly to the specifications when producing cards.

Use the gradient Pantone® logo in 6DP6.®

Cards should be printed on Mohawk Navajo, Brilliant White, 130 lb. com or an equivalent stock.

3.5"

.5"

2.14"

1.07"

1.07"

DAVID CALAB
Chief Exec
dcalabri
T 7
C

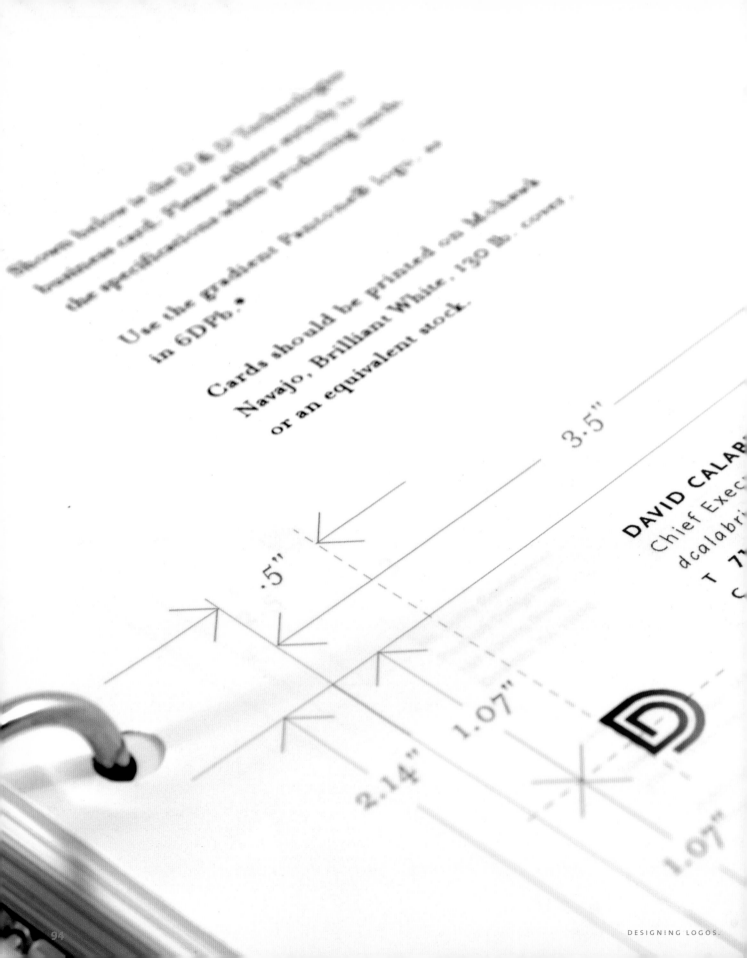

Line 1 / Name / 7/10 Scale Sans Bold / Tracking...
Line 2 / Title / 7/10 Scale Sans Regular / Tracking...
Line 3 / e-mail address / 7/10 (TT 6 p.) Scale Sans Bold / Tracking...
Line 4 / Telephone / 7/10 (TT 6 p.) Scale Sans Regular / Tracking...
Line 5 / Cell / 7/10 (C 6 p.) Scale Sans Bold / Tracking...
Line 6 / Fax / 7/10 (TT 6 p. Bold) Scale Sans Corp / Tracking...
Line 7 / Company Name / 7/10 Scale Sans Regular / Tracking...
"USA, INC." 6/10 Scale Sans Regular / Tracking...
Line 8 / Address Line 1 / 7/10 Scale Sans Regular / Tracking...
Line 9 / Address Line 2 / 7/10 Scale Sans Regular / Tracking...
Line 10 / url / 7/10 Scale Sans Italic / Tracking...
Line 11 / 800 Number / 7/10 (TT 6 p.) Scale Sans B...
Line 12 / Tag Line / 6/10 Scale Sans B...

...fficer
...echusa.com
...1300
...77 1300
...4 677 1299

D&D TECHNOLOGIES USA, INC.
7731 Woodwind Drive,
Huntington Beach, CA 92647
www.ddtechglobal.com
T 800 716 0888
Hi-Performance Hardware

Shown here are two pages from the D & D Technologies standards manual. The logo was designed by Chris Werner in 2005. In the case of both the business card and the letterhead, there is a detailed diagram showing how the items are constructed. Also included are callouts on type and color specifications. In the case of the letterhead, preprinted items are labeled, and measurements indicate proper placement of the letter contents such as the date, inside address, and letter body.

most enduring marks, foremost among them simplicity. Basic geometric shapes seem to be common in classical logos. Adequate weight and openness, balance, a sense of self-confidence (not self-consciousness), and directness can often be found.

Other characteristics that make good logos special are distinctiveness, conceptual depth, relevance, versatility, multicultural understanding, self-containment, attractiveness, legibility, memorability, and endurance. The more of these qualities present in the logo, the more likely it will endure and, in doing so, be of greater value to that which it represents.

Creating good design is challenging, and good logo design is even more so. Along with good design comes the pleasure of knowing you've done the job well. There are few design-related experiences more gratifying than driving along a road, seeing a logo you designed many years ago, and knowing it has held up well and is still working effectively. Validation from those who have benefited from your design makes it that much more special. For me, the only way to trump that sense of accomplishment, pride, and pleasure was hearing an excited little voice in the backseat saying, "Daddy, look, your logo!"

OPPOSITE: The Image Works logo was designed in 2006 by Jack Gernsheimer. As the design process evolved (see pages 200–205), the mark became symmetrical. Once I felt it had "fully cooked" I became concerned that it was a bit mechanical and needed an infusion of soul. When the distressing was applied and the stamplike appearance emerged, I felt that it improved in two ways. First, it had a more organic, lively, and visually appealing look. Second, the stamp appearance gave the symbol a more validating quality.

When the logo's handlers kept wanting to "clean it up," we recognized the need to emphasize that the surface was meant to be textured and shouldn't be altered.

On the left are 9 colors which can be used as a secondary palette. Listed beneath each stamp is the CMYK breakdown, to be used for print applications, and RGB for web and other monitor applications. Below is the *default* Red logo, with Pantone® number included.

STEEL BLUE:
C64.M23.Y0.K29
R66.G107.B140

LIGHT BLUE:
C64.M23.Y0.K0
R94.G150.B197

LIGHT TEAL:
C64.M23.Y41.K0
R94.G145.B127

BRONZE:
C21.M46.Y100.K12
R177.G109.B4

GOLD:
C11.M29.Y93.K0
R227.G172.B4

ORANGE:
C13.M68.Y93.K0
R221.G78.B15

RED (Default):
C0.M79.Y100.K0
R255.G54.B0
Pantone® 179

CHARTREUSE:
C14.M9.Y96.K0
R219.G217.B19

LEAF GREEN:
C36.M9.Y95.K0
R163.G193.B30

OLIVE:
C36.M30.Y97.K0
R163.G149.B21

Below is a 2 color and Black & White break down. No matter which logo configuration is used, the tones should be used consistently as shown.

2 COLOR:
"The & Works": 45% Black
"Image": 100% Black
Stamp and "i" dot: Pantone® 179

BLACK & WHITE:
"The & Works": 45% Black
"Image": 100% Black
Stamp and "i" dot: 65% Black

01   02   03

TO GAIN AN UNDERSTANDING OF WHAT IT TAKES FOR A LOGO TO ENDURE,

NOTHING BEATS OBSERVING CLASSICAL LOGOS. Like music, literature, and any other

art form, longevity results from a job superbly done. Additionally, there's often an

enigmatic presence giving the work a rightness, as if it were meant to be. While

conventional works become dated or less appealing over time, classics continue to

look and sound wonderful every time you see or hear them. In the following pages,

you'll see scores of logos that are either proven classics due to their longevity or

exhibit qualities that all but ensure eventual classic status.

STEINWAY & SONS

1865

1875

Steinway & Sons

Steinway & Sons has been manufacturing outstanding pianos since 1853. The original logo,
conceived by William Steinway, was first seen
on key lids in 1865 and was registered in 1876.
Nearly symmetrical, the logo takes advantage
of the opportunity to position two S's in a
Rorschach configuration. In doing so, and with
minimal additional activity, the symbol clearly
resembles a lyre with an ampersand placed in
the center.

   At the bottom are three foot petals, the
middle one invented by Steinway in 1875. While
there is some ornamentation added to embel-
lish and adorn the mark, the design stops short
of being frilly, and it has held up admirably
over the years. Shown are logos from 1885,
1909, 1929, and 2002. The current version was
introduced in 1955. Photos: Steinway & Sons.

Bass

The self-proclaimed "world's most famous
trademark" for Bass Ale is Britain's first registered trademark. Dating back to 1875, this is a
classic example of all options being available.
Since few nonrepresentational commercial
logos existed at the time, a shape as simple
as an equilateral triangle was available for ap-
propriation. The drawback to the use of a basic
geometric shape to represent a product is that
it is seen commonly and, taken out of context,
has no relation to the product.

1890	1898	1909

General Electric

Dow

Mercedes-Benz

The General Electric logo was designed in the 1890s. The circular shape has a timeless quality, and the inner activity near the perimeter of the circle gives a sense of motion and fluidity that is reinforced by the elegant treatment of the interconnected initials. Stylistically reminiscent of the Art Nouveau era from which it came, the logo is currently used on packaging and other applications that have a very contemporary typographic treatment. Because of the classical nature of the symbol and, particularly, its clean circular profile, the mark has a surprisingly neutral appearance that looks stylistically comfortable when juxtaposed with the most contemporary fonts and integrated into the most contemporary environments.

One can't help thinking that after being such a familiar fixture in the visual environment for over a century, the mark becomes emotionally neutral for us, making it even more broadly compatible. While clearly of another era, this classic logo still effectively adorns millions of consumer products and other applications more than a century after its inception.

The Dow diamond was created by internal designer M. B. Johnson in 1898, when the commercial bleach manufacturer began shipping product. The symbol was adopted as the company logo in 1918 and was registered in 1921. Due to the good fortune of having a three-letter name, the letters fit comfortably into the horizontally elongated diamond. From a public relations standpoint, the company fell on hard times during the Vietnam War. Despite the negative association, however, the logo endured and is still very much in use, although it appears to be used in a very small size in applications where the product brand is dominant, such as Saran Wrap®. Because of the austerity of the mark, major reduction appears to present no problems.

The Mercedes-Benz logo was designed in 1909 by Gottlieb Daimler and modified in 1988 by Kurt Weidemann. The three points represent engines operating on land, on sea, and in the air. The circle that surrounds the triangular element serves to hold together and strengthen the mark. Because of an outstanding branding effort, both the logo and the name are synonymous with utmost quality. "Oh Lord, won't you buy me a Mercedes-Benz...."

1913

1917

London Underground

BMW

The London Underground logo was designed in 1913 by Edward Johnston. Eminently recognizable, this mark has endured for nearly a century and shows no signs of being rendered ineffective. On the contrary, it is a true London icon, omnipresent and thoroughly woven into the fabric of the city. The simplest of shapes, the circle and the rectangle, work in combination with one another symmetrically. The bold primary palette of red and blue also contributes to the instant recognition of this symbol, even from a significant distance.

The BMW logo was designed in 1917 by Franz Josef Popp and modified in the 1990s by Zintzmeyer & Lux. The feature that clearly distinguishes this famous symbol is the inner circle, which is divided into quadrants. The checkerboard appearance is suggestive of crosshairs, in turn suggesting precision and primarily implying the checkered racing flag, which in and of itself represents speed and victory. Were the letters not included, this symbol would still be easily recognizable as the BMW logo.

The original Allianz logo (not shown), designed in 1890, was a complex coat of arms. The subsequent mark, introduced in 1923, dramatically stylized and simplified the earlier image while retaining the bird. The changes that occurred in the 1977 redesign were little more than the addition of an outer circle to better contain the mark. Finally, the 1999 version currently in use removes all but the most essential components necessary to keep the bird recognizable.

1923

1924

1938

Allianz

The Allianz logo was designed in 1923 by Karl Schulpig and modified in 1999 by Claus Koch. The earlier version of the logo, which represents this German-based insurance and banking giant, incorporated a simplified representation of a large bird with a shield. The later revised mark retains the stylized bird, but has beautifully reduced the symbol to little more than three vertical rules that, due to the profile of the head atop the middle rule, offer enough visual information to identify the bird.

Boehringer Ingelheim

The current Boehringer Ingelheim logo was originally designed in 1924 and was modified in 1962 and again in 1997 by MetaDesign. The first logo, used from 1893 to 1908, was contained in a vertical oval with the intertwined letters "CHBS," which stands for C. H. Boehringer and Sohn. The logo became circular in 1908. The first of the two treatments that evolved into the current mark was introduced in 1924. The logo contains a stylized interpretation of the central section of the imperial palace of Charlemagne. The graphic treatment uses seven equally spaced vertical rules—two short, three tall, two short—to simply and elegantly represent the palace. The chevron on the top clarifies that this is a roofed dwelling. By removing the name from inside the circle and allowing the rules to bleed out of the bottom of the containing circle, designer Ole Schäfer (at MetaDesign) has liberated the palace, and the relationship of the inner rules and outer circle is balanced and comfortable, with ample negative space allowing the mark to breathe.

Volkswagen

The original Volkswagen logo was designed in 1938 and refreshed in 1996 and 2000, when color blends and implied three-dimensionality were introduced. There is speculation regarding the design of the mark. One theory states that the logo was created by Franz Reimspeiss, a Porsche employee, while another credits Martin Freyer with winning a design competition. Either way, this is arguably one of the most successful logos ever designed. The two letters seem to interact perfectly with one another, and the circle of the same line weight contains the letters with just the right amount of "air" in the negative spaces to retain legibility.

1951

1959

Columbia Broadcasting System

Westinghouse

The CBS eye, designed by William Golden, is the embodiment of the logo that endures. Illustrated by Golden's associate, Kurt Weihs, the mark was introduced by Columbia Broadcasting System in 1951. The symbol heralded the emergence of television over radio as the preeminent medium in the broadcast industry. Inspired by the elegant simplicity of mid-nineteenth-century Shaker design, Golden introduced a modified form of Didot Bodoni, which he'd encountered in France, to typographically complement the symbol. The font's unusual range of thicks to thins gives it a contemporary and classically elegant flair.

While icons representing the human eye have been around for millennia, few have distilled it to such an efficient yet immediately identifiable form. Comprised entirely of circular elements, this perfectly balanced mark epitomizes transcendence of fashion. When Golden set out to design a new symbol for the next season in 1952, CBS President Frank Stanton had no intention of replacing the eye, saying, "Just when you're beginning to be bored with what you've done, is when it's beginning to be noticed by your audience."

The Westinghouse logo was designed in 1959 by Paul Rand, in collaboration with architect Eliot Noyes, Herbert Matter, and Charles Eames. It's hard to imagine one symbol with so much all-star input. The results show that this symbol looks fresh nearly half a century later. Why? Because clean, direct simplicity almost always trumps complexity.

Sparingly using two line weights, there is ample shift from the thick, round-ended line and circles to the lighter-weight lines that describe the *W* and the circle. There is far more visual distinctiveness and appeal than monotonal line weight would have had. The suggestion of circuitry and modernity add conceptual depth to this elegant masterpiece.

1960

1960

ca. 1960

Canadian National Railway

When asked how long he felt the Canadian National Railway logo would endure, Toronto designer Allan Fleming predicted "fifty years, at least." In fact, the logo he designed in 1960 is well on its way to surpassing that prediction. Collaborating with New York art director James Valkus, Fleming spent months working on the project, partially because his father had been a longtime employee of CNR, which added a sentimental component to the project.

The fluid, rounded, linked characters met with some controversy for departing from the then-traditional treatment of railroad logos. Subsequently, the logo has influenced many designs, likely including that of the universally recognized CNN logo designed some twenty years later.

Chase Manhattan Bank

The Chase Manhattan Bank logo, designed in 1960 by Tom Geismar, is reminiscent of a Möbius strip. It is two-dimensional but appears to twist and show two sides rather than one. An added dimension is introduced by way of the square center, which has an appearance similar to that of a coin from China's Han Empire, dating back to between 200 B.C. to 200 A.D. The use of gaps serves to separate the shapes, keeping the mark cohesive and suggesting strength by virtue of interweaving. The octagonal silhouette adds distinctiveness and facilitates quick recognition. This mark was an early entry in the field of nonliteral American logos and helped blaze the trail for many to follow.

Emissionzentrale Schweizer Lokalbanken

The Emissionzentrale Schweizer Lokalbanken logo interlocks an ambiguous shape that is repeated, rotating 120 degrees each of three times, to form a triangular element. The tightly woven configuration, along with the bold weight of the central elements, suggests a sense of solidity and strength to the symbol representing this financial institution. The logo was created by Swiss designer Marcel Wyss.

1960

1960

Quebec Hydro Electric

International Paper

The logo for Quebec Hydro Electric, designed in 1960 by Gagnon Valkus, employs the hardworking lightning bolt, used repeatedly to represent all things electric. This is one of those rare instances when employing overused imagery is arguably the right thing to do. First, the bolt is widely understood. More importantly, it's the perfect element to complete the letter *Q*. Capitalizing on this opportunity is nearly irresistible, and it's hard to fault the designer when the end result exhibits so many qualities of a great logo.

Designed in 1960 by Lester Beall, the classic International Paper logo embodies the monotonal simplicity and directness of that generation of logo design. The outer line encircles the treelike element constructed of the letters *I* and *P*, making the mark self-contained and cohesive. Additionally, the mark is accessible and friendly, yet ever sophisticated.

1961   1961   1962

KLM   World Wildlife Fund   Jack L. Larsen

The KLM logo was designed in 1961 by F. H. K. Henrion and modified in 1991 by Chris Ludlow at Hyperlink. The stylized crown is composed of four circles, a line, and a plus. It adds a regal touch to the logo for Royal Dutch Airlines by "crowning" the initials. The crown's simplified treatment makes the overall logo recognizable and universally understood.

The World Wildlife Fund logo was designed in 1961 by Peter Scott. There are few creatures that have the universal appeal of a young panda, and WWF likely recognized the fund-raising potential of adopting this symbol as its logo. According to Scott, an ornithologist and artist, "We wanted an animal that is beautiful, is endangered, and is one loved by many people in the world for its enduring qualities."

Stylized and distilled, there's an efficiency of line, shape, and color working to keep the mark spare, yet highly recognizable and friendly.

Jack Lenor Larsen's highly communicative logo represents the textile designer with universal clarity. No matter where you live on the planet, this symbol is clearly recognizable as interwoven strands.

Designed in 1962 by Arnold Saks and James S. Ward, the bold horizontal and vertical bands intertwine to suggest woven textiles produced by Larsen, whose choice of color and pattern strongly influenced modern textile design. By having a gap wherever horizontals and verticals meet, an illusion of three-dimensionality results. While this technique is not uncommon, it is used with effective simplicity and clarity in this enduringly contemporary mark. The logo also achieves a sense of unity and cooperation, characteristics desired by every company.

1960s

ca. 1962

1962

Turin Kala Oy

The logo for the Finnish fish cannery Turin Kala Oy, designed by Bror Zetterborg, effectively combines playfulness with sophistication. The minimalistic representation offers just enough visual information to unmistakably identify the four leaping fish. The unfortunate appearance of the swastika in the negative space is mitigated by the rounded treatment and the friendly dot eyes. The inclusion of the dorsal fin, so simply executed, is critical to the legibility of the mark.

American Broadcasting Company

The ABC logo, designed in 1962 by Paul Rand, is a classic example of simplicity at work. The symbol is comprised of a perfect circle, arguably the most enduring of all shapes, and contains three circular lowercase letters, which are strongly reminiscent of the Bauhaus font, designed by Herbert Bayer at the Dessau Bauhaus in 1925. The lowercase letters are themselves comprised of nearly perfect circles and are arranged side by side. Care was taken to space the letters equally, both visually and physically. The inner circles that are the resulting negative shapes provide a sense of rhythm and balance, and while the overall symbol is symmetrical, the inner activity is not.

The circle is a shape that will never go in or out of fashion. The use of the circular Bauhaus-like characters echoes the circular shape of the containing circle and creates a mark with balance and rhythm, which will endure to serve the company for as long as it is called upon to do so.

![Alcoa logo]

1962

1963

1963

Chrysler Corporation

Koninklijke Hoogovens

Alcoa

The Chrysler Corporation logo, designed in 1962 by Lippincott & Margulies and referred to as the "Pentastar," is a pentagon, made unique because it is constructed of five nonequilateral triangles rotating at seventy-two degrees around a central point. In the resulting negative space is a five-pointed star. Because of the separation and the squat configuration of the basic triangular elements, the star has a distinctively thin appearance as it bleeds out of the pentagon, making it look sleeker than the conventional star shape. In the auto industry, sleek suggests speed, and speed is good.

The Koninklijke Hoogovens logo was designed in 1963 by Jurriaan Schrofer. Note the similarities between this steel-and-metals company logo and the Chrysler Corporation pentagon. The difference, other than the obviously thinner star, is that the star in one of the logos is the by-product of a convergence of triangles and, in the other logo, of diamondlike shapes.

The Alcoa logo was designed in 1963 by Saul Bass and minimally modified in 1998 by Arnold Saks. The uniquely stylized letter *A* is constructed of three equal-sized diamonds, the uppermost of which has its lower half removed. The box in which the letter resides is softened by the generously radiused corners.

Alcoa's first corporate mark appeared in 1894, when Alcoa was still known as the Pittsburgh Reduction Company. The original mark—a cross over a circle, along with the company's initials and the word "aluminum"—was used for thirty-five years with only slight modification.

1963

1964

El Al

Met Life

The El Al logo was designed in 1963 by Otto Treumann. Both the English and Hebrew characters have an extended, monotonal, and confident look and feel. The letters are customized to fit comfortably into one another. The result of the combination of letters is an extreme horizontal format. More importantly, the viewer has a sense of security because of the solid, yet energized, forward-leaning appearance. The colors, Pantone® 280 Blue and Cool Grey 6, lend a soothing quality to the identity.

The Met Life logo, designed in 1964 by Don Ervin, uses as its central element the letter *M*, or the letters *M* and *L*, depending on how you observe it. This mark's visual impact is created by the dynamic starlike activity that takes place within the negative space. By chopping off the top of the letters, they become more distinctive and original, as well as more energetic. This long-lived symbol has kept its fresh appearance for decades. Granted, it got lots of help in 1985 from Charlie Brown's dog Snoopy, who served as a mascot for many years, adding familiarity and friendliness to the insurance giant's image.

Mobil

1964

1964

1964

Mobil

Woolmark

Mitsubishi

The Mobil logo was designed around 1964 by Chermayeff and Geismar. Fortunately, the familiar Pegasus was retained for selective use to preserve equity and add visual appeal when used in conjunction with the classical Futura-based logotype. The simple switch to a red o in the blue name works very effectively to distinguish the word. The letters, tightly spaced in a fashion reminiscent of that period, give the name a sense of cohesiveness and strength without compromising legibility.

Because of the timeless simplicity of the treatment of the name, motion and activity, such as sloshing gasoline, was sometimes shown within the center of the letter.

The Woolmark logo was designed by Francesco Seraglio in 1964. Configured in the fashion of a Möbius strip, the grouping of three elements appears to intertwine like a skein of wool. The overall shape is soft yet stable, by virtue of the secure base of the triangle and the generously radiused points. The reflection of positive and negative shapes and spaces allows for detail without compromising reduction capability. This mark remains compellingly friendly and contemporary after more than four decades.

The current Mitsubishi logo appears to have surfaced in 1964. The shipping company that was formed in the 1870s and later became Mitsubishi used a triangular water chestnut on its ships' flags. "Mitsu" means three and "bishi" means water chestnut. The three-diamond mark used today emerged as a reinterpretation of the family crest of the founder.

The three diamonds are arranged to form an equilateral triangle. They suggest a highly stylized floral representation, and have balance and symmetry. The negative space works to lighten and distinguish the logo. There's a suggestion of convergence as well as outward movement.

ca. 1965

ca. 1965

Centre d'Esthetique Industrielle

Boise Cascade

Whether intentional or not, this symbol representing the Centre d'Esthetique Industrielle (Center of Industrial Design) in Sofia, Bulgaria, has visual characteristics very similar to those in the CBS "eye" (see page 104). Designed by Stephan Kantscheff, this example illustrates one of the few downsides of simplicity, where the minimalist representation of the human eye utilizes three basic shapes, the central one being a perfect circle, and thus shares much in common with William Golden's classic 1951 icon.

The Boise Cascade logo designed in the 1960s depicts a pine tree within the containing circle. The Idaho-based manufacturer of wood and paper-related products chose this imagery because trees are the source of lumber as well as the pulp needed to manufacture paper, and the green color supports the image. The upward chevrons infuse a sense of growth and stability. One could also argue that they represent downward-turned, cascading branches, though it's not certain that either suggestion reflects the designer's intent. The monotonal line weight, commonly used in the sixties, gives the logo a simple yet graphically powerful appearance and retains its contemporary quality. The proportion of positive and negative shapes and spaces, as well as the symmetry, give the symbol balance. The simplicity of detail allows the mark to be painted on relatively rough-surfaced products such as plywood sheets without significant loss of legibility.

1965

Chicago Pharmaceutical

The Chicago Pharmaceutical logo designed by John Massey in 1965 suggests a serpent that has the general shape of the caduceus, based on the Hermetic astrological principle of using the planets and stars to heal the sick. In recent times, the caduceus has become associated with the practice of medicine. Some medical organizations join the serpents of the caduceus with rungs to suggest a DNA double-helix. Massey executed this concept with simple elegance, creating the letters *C* and *P* out of the serpent. By doing this, there is an immediate association with medicine, and the letters themselves have a distinctively original and contemporary appearance.

Seatrain Lines

The Seatrain Lines logo was designed in 1965 by Tom Geismar. It's readily apparent that the two positive arrows represent the distribution of cargo to and from locations. What's less blatant is the letter *S* formed by the negative space between the arrows, whose heads are carefully sized to help define the inner letter. The consistency of both positive and negative line weights gives all three elements in this symbol a sense of equality. The fact that the ends of the arrows are squared off rather than rounded gives the initial a solid and distinctive appearance.

Bendix Corporation

The Bendix Corporation began manufacturing automotive brake systems in 1924 and has diversified into other areas such as aeronautics hydraulics and consumer appliances. The current logo was designed in 1966 by Lippincott & Margulies. The bold, condensed sans serif font gives the logotype a sense of mass and implied strength. While the dynamic concave shape beneath the name is somewhat reminiscent of a brake pad, it is general enough not to alienate other product areas. The upward sweep of the arc, which widens slightly as it moves to the right, gives the identity a sense of positive momentum. There is also a play on the name, as the arc "bends" upward.

1966

ca. **1968**

Cubic Metre

The Cubic Metre logo was designed for the U.K.-based furniture company in 1966 by Minale Tattersfield & Partners. There are a number of clever devices at work in this deceptively sophisticated mark. Most obviously, the large lowercase *m* is turned on its side, reduced, and placed in the upper right-hand space next to the letter so that it reads as *m* to the third power. The retention of the same character, reduced, exhibits a sense of confidence and credits the viewer with the ability to recognize its clear similarity to the numeral *3*. There was added significance to the mark, since the metric system had only recently been introduced in the United Kingdom. Additionally, all three of the founders had the initial *M*. This mark exemplifies the enduring effectiveness of smart, understated design.

New Jersey Transit

The New Jersey Transit logo capitalizes on the ability to neatly fit the *N* into the *J*. The highly stylized letters would be nearly illegible and disturbingly proportioned if they were standing alone, yet together, they support one another and read clearly. The white gap separating the letters looks like the center stripe on a divided road, reinforcing the fact that the service NJT provides is ground transportation.

FILA

1969

1969

ca. 1970

Eastwood Spices

The logo for Eastwood Spices was designed in 1969 by Jack Gernsheimer. As the designer, I wanted to explore characters that had a generally Asian appearance. The resulting letters looked as if they'd been painted with a bamboo brush.

As the *E* and *S* developed, I became aware of a distinct leaflike image emerging in the negative space. With much refinement, both positive and negative shapes became more visible and balanced. The resulting silhouette was a bold radiused square, greatly lightened by the openness of the inner spaces.

De Staats Mijnen

The DSM logo was designed in 1969 by an internal designer. The mark exemplifies the geometrically based nonfigurative symbol representing many European companies of that era. The acronym stands for De Staats Mijnen, aka Dutch State Mines, even though Dutch mining ended in 1973.

The hexagonal center is surrounded by three elements that create an outer hexagon, suggesting components encircling a core. This seems a valid, if ambiguous, symbol to represent the multifaceted company DSM has become.

Fila

The Fila brothers started manufacturing clothing in 1911, in the shadow of the Italian Alps. The current logo has been used effectively, largely because of the treatment of the letter *F*. The red bar makes the initial unique and highly memorable. Additionally, the snakelike letters, not unlike NASA's (see page 119), have a futuristic look that's aged surprisingly well. Most importantly, the logo has been worn by many of the world's finest athletes, reinforcing a highly successful branding effort.

The company began in Auburn, New York, in 1889 as Bundy Manufacturing Company, and became known as International Time Recording Company (ITR).

In 1891, a Dayton, Ohio, manufacturer purchased patents and began producing a new type of commercial scale under the name Computing Scale Company (CSC).

In 1911, CSC, ITR, and Tabulating Machine Company merged into Computing-Tabulating-Recording Company, not exactly a name that rolls off the tongue.

Recognizing this, the company was renamed International Business Machines Corporation in 1924. The new logo depicted a globe rung with the word "International."

The "globe" logo served the company for twenty-two years, and in January 1947, a much simplified and contemporary logotype was introduced, consisting of the three square-serif letters "IBM" taken from the font Beton Bold.

In 1956, legendary graphic designer Paul Rand was commissioned to update the logotype, clearly respecting the equity the earlier version had amassed, helping the punch-card tabulating company to usher in computers. The font Rand selected to influence the modified characters was City Medium, giving the emerging giant a look of strength and solidity.

Rand was called upon again in 1972 to freshen the now-familiar mark, and the eight-striped logo, suggestive of "speed and dynamism," continues to serve the company to this day.

Initially, a thirteen-striped version of the logo was also produced, but it is no longer in use.

In the final eight-stripe version, the height of the serif was likely used to determine the height of the positive and negative stripes. Rand felt no need to directly describe the negative spaces; instead, he allowed them to be implicitly defined by their relationship to the positive shapes. This treatment went on to influence many future marks that tried to convey a sense of motion with static imagery. While the style became cliché, this mark endures nobly.

olivetti

1970s

ca. 1970

1970

Target

The Target logo is a classic example of simplicity at work. Granted, the logo's designer lucked out when it came to creating a logo with obvious imagery, but the concentric circle-within-a-circle interpretation of a target is brilliantly simple and communicates universally. Care was clearly given to determining the thickness of negative space, which is the third ring on the target.

The red-and-white palette carries the simplicity from shape to color, and is used with great success in the overall brand imagery. Whether used independently, with accompanying type, in a repetitive pattern, or in other ways, such as the ring around a dog's eye, this mark is highly recognizable and identifiable in or out of a contextual environment.

Olivetti

The Olivetti logotype was designed by Walter Ballmer. The Italian company began manufacturing typewriters in 1908. The original logo, designed by Camillo Olivetti, was reworked by Xanti Schawinsky, Giovanni Pintori, and Marcello Nizzoli before being redesigned in 1970 by Ballmer.

The Olivetti logotype achieves its cohesiveness from the tight packing of the eight letters, with their short, equal-length ascenders. The dots of the i's have a shape suggestive of a typewriter key. The radiused corners of the lowercase characters give them a more friendly and accessible appearance, while the unique treatment of the letter e lends a degree of distinctive originality to this enduring logotype.

1972

1972

1972

| Swiss Federal Railways | IBM | Lithographix |

The Swiss Federal Railways logo was designed in 1972 by Hans Hartmann and modified in 1978 by Josef Müller-Brockmann and Peter Spalinger. Given Switzerland's reputation for precision, one must assume that the national train system, known as Schweizerische Bundesbahnen, exemplifies efficiency. This logo reflects that quality, using the white cross in the red field, which is similar in content, if not in weight, to the Swiss flag. The arrowheads, while often cliché, integrate visually and conceptually to suggest movement and transport. This mark has an appealing sense of understatement that seems totally appropriate to that which it represents.

The IBM logotype, designed by Paul Rand in 1972, has a history nearly as colorful as the corporation it represents.

The Lithographix logo, designed in 1972 by Dan Hanrahan and art directed by Don Weller and Dennis Juett, treats the letter L in a unique and powerful way. The curved stem of the character represents the drum of an offset printing press, and the horizontal base is created by the suggestion of ink being offset onto paper. The prominent inclusion of the gradiant halftone screens makes the mark visually interesting, aesthetically appealing, and relevant to the offset printing company it represents. The halftone image was hand drawn and wrapped around an oatmeal package to achieve the curved effect. It was then photographed, retouched, and manipulated. While halftone gradients have been commonly used, few if any treatments have incorporated the motif more elegantly or distinctively.

1972

1973

National Penn Bank

In 1972, the National Bank of Boyertown was about to celebrate its one-hundredth anniversary. The growing institution commemorated the occasion by building a new corporate headquarters. Given that the bank's "logo" at the time was a picture of the time/temperature clock, the bank president recognized the need to create a better symbol. The triple objective was to give the symbol a feeling of growth, local color, and stability.

The stylized tulip, designed by Jack Gernsheimer, acknowledged floral imagery prevalent in local Pennsylvania Dutch culture. It also represented growth, which was suggested not only in the flower but also in the negative shape that emerged. The cropping that created a square base gave stability to the symbol.

When the bank grew and underwent a name change, the National Penn Bank kept the tulip logo, and the transition was seamless, with little or no loss in the equity gained by years of goodwill and exposure.

Deutsche Bank

The Deutsche Bank logo was designed in 1973 by the highly respected graphic designer Anton Stankowski. In the simplest of terms, this symbol, by virtue of the bold linear box, suggests a great deal of protection for the inner element. The slanted line within the box leans boldly forward, offering a sense of positive momentum. The combination of the two components gives a strong sense of security combined with growth, thus addressing the universal wish of the investor.

1974

1974

1974

Berks County Prison Society

Buhrmann

NASA

Designed in 1974 by Jack Gernsheimer, this symbol for a local prison advocacy group shows two starkly simplified figures shaking hands. The vertical rules represent prison bars, and the tight spacing intentionally suggests a sense of confinement. The figure outside the bars represents the community at large (as well as the at-large community) extending itself to the incarcerated community. There is also a secondary suggestion of a smiling face, giving the mark a subliminally friendly feel.

The Buhrmann logo was designed in 1974 by Pieter van den Busken and revised in 1998 by DG Design. The customized Möbius-like symbol sets up a sense of momentum in the shape appearing in the negative space. The nonfigurative mark ambiguously represents this Amsterdam-based office supply products giant, which has merged and grown since 1851.

The NASA logo designed by Danne and Blackburn met with some unfortunate bureaucratic resistance when it replaced the original (1959) NASA "meatball" logo in 1974. The "worm," as it was not-so-affectionately called, was a favorite in the design community but was not so warmly embraced among NASA directors. *Houston, we have a problem.* In 1992, a new director, claiming "the magic is back," chose to replace the worm with the meatball, abandoning the fine work of a duly selected and most worthy design team.

The NASA logotype, which wisely reduces the agency name to its familiar acronym, has a look that is appropriately progressive without being falsely futuristic. The monotonal weight of the characters blends smoothly with the curved junctions, and the central ligature allows the tight letterspacing to remain consistent and cohesive. The *A*'s strongly suggest a rocket's nose cone and gain thrust and distinctiveness thanks to the omission of the crossbars.

1975

1977

United Technologies

In 1975, United Aircraft changed their name to United Technologies "to connote the breadth of its products, markets, and activities." Many of the products they produced still related to flight, including jet engines first manufactured by Pratt & Whitney in 1948.

The logo is loosely suggestive of a turbine engine and of UT's Sikorsky Helicopter, with thinning lines giving the mark a distinct sense of motion. The lines thin as they rotate clockwise from three o'clock, allowing the outer negative space to open and create secondary activity similar to that of a nautilus shell. The inner circle opens and lightens the mark, also giving it a more distinct overall appearance.

3M

The 3M logo, designed by Siegel+Gale in 1977, is solid, massive, and classical. The choice of this bold weight of Helvetica in bright red gives 3M, a self-proclaimed innovator, a sense of stability coupled with innovational spirit. The overlap of the characters, caused by supertight kerning, adds to the strength and cohesiveness of the mark and to the perception of the company it represents. Shown above are many of the previous 3M logos that blazed the trail for the current mark.

1977

1977

1978

Apple Computer

Nedlloyd

Girl Scouts

The original Apple Computer logo, designed by Rob Janoff at Regis McKenna Advertising in 1977, combined imagery of an apple and a rainbow. The "byte" taken out of the right-hand side of the apple added to the playfulness of the colorful mark. Thanks to the inherent strength of the overall shape, with its pleasing curves and straightforward legibility, the mark did not suffer and, in fact, arguably benefited from the removal of the multicolored palette.

Later treatments of the mark included a simple Pantone® 429 grey silhouette and, after that, a dimensional gel-like appearance.

The Nedlloyd logo was designed in 1977 by Studio Groen. The image resembles a secure knot, which is highly appropriate for a shipping line. The thick, intertwined strands give the sense that the items being shipped will be delivered unharmed. The mark has strength because of line weight and the interrelation-ship of the elements, and the forty-five-degree angle offers interesting possibilities for the logo/logotype lockups.

The Girl Scouts' logo designed by Saul Bass in 1978 has an outer shape retained from its predecessor dating back to 1914, allowing the organization to capitalize on the logo's equity and recognition. The two negative inner shapes and the positive shape between them form silhouettes of three girls' profiles. The light-dark-light color shifts speak of the diversity of the membership, while the stylized profiles have a simple yet clear feminine appearance. The resulting shape on the left-hand side of the mark is suggestive of a girl's hair. The logo has a sense of balance, and the forward-leaning figures give it a progressive, nonstatic quality.

swissair

1970s–1980s   1978   1979

Swissair   Hahn Fire Apparatus

The Swissair logo, designed in 1978 by Karl   The logo for Hahn Fire Apparatus was designed
Gerstner, works on a number of levels. The   by Jack Gernsheimer in 1979. This mark, while
alignment of the white "plus" with the char-   seemingly simple, incorporates a significant
acter height of the logotype gives a sense of   amount of imagery. "Hahn" is German for
visual appeal as well as Swiss orderliness. The rooster, and the logo depicts a stylized rooster
red parallelogram, a geometric shape that is   head in profile view. The red comb atop the
simple and classic without being overworked,   head is illustrated in flamelike fashion,
resembles an airplane's tail fin, while the shape representing fire. The gullet beneath the bill
effectively holds the plus, gives a sense of mo- resembles a drop of water, which is a funda-
mentum, and is memorable because it's used   mental ingredient in firefighting. Stylistically,
infrequently. The lowercase logotype gives a   the combination of near-square and circular
more friendly and accessible appearance.   shapes keeps this logo looking fresh and
                                                contemporary.

| 1980 | ca. 1980 | 1981 |

Cable News Network

New Holland

Texaco

Cable News Network revolutionized the way news was presented on television. Begun in 1980, CNN offered news junkies 24/7 access to the top stories of the day.

New Holland is an Italy-based multinational manufacturer of agricultural and construction equipment. Over the decades, the company has expanded and changed its product line. The logo, which was previously used by Fiatagri, was adopted by New Holland in 1993. Through mergers, acquisitions, and changes, the symbol that has assured loyal customers of continuing reliability and quality has been the blue "leaf" logo. The distinct shape of the mark, a cross between an oval and a radiused vertical rect-angle, makes it recognizable even in a purely silhouette form, as one might see it from a distance. Add the leaf vein component and you have a symbol that strongly implies growth, be it in crop fields or in monetary value. Both positive and negative shapes within the mark reinforce this desirable perception.

Texaco first introduced the red five-pointed star in 1903. In 1907, the star was placed in a circle, and a capital T was introduced in 1909. In 1981, after several additional iterations, the current logo was designed by Anspach Grossman and Portugal. The star seemed a good choice for a symbol, given Texaco's association with the Lone Star State.

The logo is comprised of ligature upon ligature, connecting the three letters and suggesting a sense of the continuation present in the news programming format. The inline that divides the letters in half adds visual interest and openness to the characters. While the letters hold together and flow well, there is a compromise in legibility. The letters could be read as "CMI" or "CNV" if done in a style remi-niscent of Herb Lubalin's Avant Garde Gothic. Conversely, the predecessor logo likely to have influenced the mark, Canadian National Railway, has two connected letters that read clearly and decisively.

The five-pointed star within the circle marries two pure geometric shapes and gives the logo symmetry and balance. The centered letter personalizes the logo, which is widely recognized in more than 150 countries.

1982

1983

Sun Microsystems

The Sun Microsystems logo was designed in 1982 by Vaughan Pratt. The diamond-shaped symbol holds a surprise not usually seen in this ambigram at first glance. The fundamental component that initially appears to be a stylized letter *S* also reads as a *U* and an *N*, spelling out the word "SUN." The symbol is actually four diamonds within a large diamond. The radiused corners resulting from the simple rounded characters serve to soften this clever and enduring mark.

Pfaltzgraff

The Pfaltzgraff logo was designed in 1983 by Jack Gernsheimer. The logo was fashioned after the Pfaltz Castle in Germany. As the designer, I chose to take liberties and make the castle symmetrical. Rather than remain representational, the stylized mark enlarges and balances the window and door areas. Extreme simplification was necessary because the primary function of the mark is to be pressed into the back of ceramic dinnerware pieces prior to firing. The modified oval gives the symbol a distinctive silhouette when compared to the much more commonly used circle.

1984

ca. 1984

1984

Public Broadcasting System

The logo for Public Broadcasting System was designed by Chermayeff and Geismar around 1984. Its predecessor used the initials "PBS," with the *P* resembling a face. The revised logo eliminates initials but retains the head and the suggestion of a *P*. The enlarged eye suggests that sight is the primary sense impacted by PBS programming. The multiple faces support the idea of service to the public. Like the treatment in the Girl Scouts logo (see page 121), there is also a suggestion of multiculturalism because of the color change in the center face.

Saturn

The logo for GM's emerging automobile division Saturn was introduced around 1984. Always set within a red rectangle, the intersecting circular and oval lines, which bleed out of the box, represent the spherical planet and its encircling rings. This is due to the widening of the line toward the bottom, adding perspective and dimension.

While it may not read as well taken out of context, the mark uses only two lines to describe the unique planet most efficiently.

Musée d'Orsay

The Musée d'Orsay logo was designed in 1984 by Jean Widmer and Bruno Monguzzi and modified in 1986 by Jean Widmer. The use of the typeface Walbaum, which has a strong resemblance to Didot, introduces exaggerated thicks and thins to add visual appeal and elegance to the mark. While available for use as stand-alone letters, in the default version the letters bleed boldly out of the top and bottom of a box in a fashion that allows the viewer to complete the picture. Taking that a step further, the apostrophe implies the presence of the *d* that precedes it.

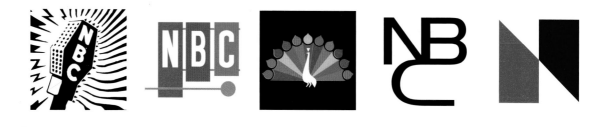

NBC

ca. 1985

1986

The Gap

The Gap is another example of a logo that
works well within a box. In this case, what's
more distinctive than the deep blue rectangle
is the widely spaced, ultracondensed serif font.
No bells and whistles here; it simply works,
year after year, to represent the specialty
clothing retailer with consistency and clarity.
You can see and recognize this logo from a mile
away.

National Broadcasting Company

Steff Geisbuhler redesigned John Graham's
peacock thirty years after the original bird
colored TV screens across the country. Instead
of eleven feathers, the number was reduced to
six, representing the divisions of the network.
The bird is flopped so it looks forward, and the
peacock's body is created from the negative
space carved out of the inner feathers. The
bird's bill, cut out of one plume, smartly and
simply defines the peacock. The color palette
of nearly primary and secondary colors adds
pizzazz to the mark.

The logo for the National Broadcasting Company has been through significant changes on its way to assuming its current peacock form. NBC's earliest logo, introduced in 1943, was a microphone. The accompanying lightning bolts are believed to have been borrowed from parent company RCA. The three chime notes, first heard on NBC Radio in 1927, accompanied the "xylophone" logo of 1954.

The original peacock, designed in 1956 by John Graham, was used to introduce color broadcasts. The peacock went from static to animated in 1957.

The "snake" logo came on the scene in 1959 and departed in 1975. It was animated, and the field behind it changed color as the familiar chimes played. Problems ensued in 1975 when a highly simplified and stylized N logo was found to conflict with an existing logo for Nebraska ETV Network. The issue was resolved and NBC used their red-and-blue version for a number of years. That logo was arguably the most graphically sophisticated of the lot, but the earlier peacock reemerged in a refined and much improved form in 1986.

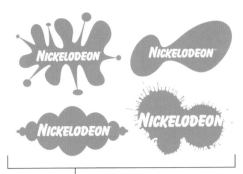

ca. 1986

Nickelodeon

Like its sister company before it, Nickelodeon helped usher in the age of alternate logos tied together by a common element. Candy Kugel, a director involved in the MTV logo's development in 1981, has said, "[The MTV logo by Manhattan Design] was totally asymmetrical, as far away from the peacock or an eye as you could get."

The Nickelodeon logo, by comparison, is conservative. Because the obliqued, rounded, and friendly logotype consistently reverses out of orange blobs that vary in shape, the mark meets the challenge of looking fresh and varied yet consistent and instantly recognizable. The MTV and Nick identity systems get high marks not for following the rules, but for breaking them.

1987

Pfizer

The Pfizer logo was designed in 1987 by Gene Grossman. In a fashion similar to but preceding GlaxoSmithKline, the symbol had a shape reminiscent of a medicine tablet. The oval shape is less often used than the circle, adding distinctiveness. The letter *f* has even more prominence than the initial cap *P*. I worked on a logo that offered the same phonetic challenge. My client Pfaltzgraff (see page 124) also had a silent *P*. I was drawn to the idea, as it appears Grossman was, of accentuating the *f*. By making the *f* the most prominent character, Grossman heightened its status, diminished that of the silent initial, and created visual interest and appeal.

1987

Historical Landscapes

Designed in 1987 by Jack Gernsheimer, this logo represents a landscape designer with the specialty of matching the period of the gardens with that of the dwelling. The imagery includes a noncontemporary residence and a tree. The combination of the grid and the matching windows ties the two segments together. Elements such as the door top and the dormers quietly reinforce the historical nature of the building, while the grid on the left suggests graph paper used in planning. Despite its complexity, the adherence to the square matrix gives order to the mark. The inclusion of the tree, albeit structured in appearance, softens the logo.

1987

1989

Starbucks

The original Starbucks logo was designed in 1971 by Terry Heckler. After studying old marine imagery, he came upon a Norse woodcut of an enticing two-tailed mermaid, which became the subject of the mark. In 1987, the symbol was redesigned in a more contemporary symmetrical style. The mark was once again revisited in 1992, when the mermaid was enlarged within the circle. The final mark, as we know it today, is well balanced and discreet, with navel and breasts concealed. There is a considerable amount of detail in the mark, but the use of thick lines and spaces allows the mark to hold up well when reduced. The logo exhibits a successful combination of contemporary and traditional style.

Norske Skog

Norske Skog, the Norwegian paper manufacturer, has a logo with a classically Scandinavian quality. Reminiscent of those designed by the brilliant Oslo-based designer Bruno Oldani, this mark, designed in 1989 by Engen and Harlem, keeps angles and line weights to a minimum. By doing so, the treelike figures, with their rounded edges, take on a friendly and approachable nature. The arrows, which double as trees, suggest both a sense of revitalization and a distribution of product.

nwa
NORTHWEST AIRLINES

1989

Northwest Airlines

To paraphrase Joni Mitchell, "there's something lost but something gained" with the redesign of the Northwest Airlines logo. The earlier version, designed by Landor and Associates and introduced in 1989, utilized some very sophisticated, albeit subtle, graphic devices. The circular outline served not as a superfluous containment shape, but rather as a compass-like element that, in combination with the triangle, suggested an arrowhead pointing to the northwest. In addition, the oblique letter *N* can also be read as the right-hand side of the stencilized letter *W*. Much of the multileveled imagery is lost in the updated mark, designed by TrueBrand in 2003. What was gained was a significant reduction in plane painting costs.

1990

Altana

The Altana logo was designed in 1990 by Stankowski+Duschek and modified in 2001 by Citigate Demuth. The mark representing this Germany-based manufacturer of coating and sealant-related products consists of an equilateral triangle, inside of which is another triangle with convex sides. The inner shape is rotated clockwise and bleeds out of the outer shape, creating three resulting shapes that have a sense of movement, even as the overall shape is securely rooted on the base of the triangle.

1991

Merck

The logo for pharmaceutical giant Merck was designed by Chermayeff and Geismar in 1991. Although the images are not immediately apparent, one can see two bisected pills and a capsule, generally representing the company's end product. The negative shapes resemble a mortar, in which medicine was ground with a pestle. The overall shape of the symbol is derived from the grouping of four intersecting circles creating a classic diamond configuration.

1992

1992

Time Warner Cable

You might say the Time Warner logo takes the CBS "eye" a step further, but at a cost. Along with the eye, there is also an ear integrated into the symbol, acknowledging that both sight and sound are part of the cable media experience. There is also a suggestion of dizziness in the pupil that results from the combination of the two elements. The logo was designed by Steff Geissbuhler at Chermayeff and Geismar around 1992.

Easily overlooked in this multifaceted mark is the use of a monotonal line, similar in appearance to a cable, to illustrate the components. The ratio of positive and negative shapes is balanced and functional, allowing the mark to reduce and broadcast well despite its detailed appearance.

Sonofon

The Sonofon logo was designed in 1992 by Johan Adam Linneballe and Steffen Gulmann at Eleven Danes. The Danish mobile telephone network adopted the dolphin as a symbol of boundless communication. The inclusion, in the negative space, of the small dolphin next to the large one adds playfulness, visual appeal, and dimension. Whether the smaller dolphin represents a child or a companion, it reinforces the idea of being connected to another. Shown above is the Libertel logo (see page 133).

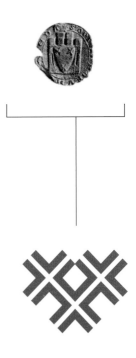

1993

1994

1994

Samsung

National Food Products

Gemeente Breda

In 1993, Samsung introduced a new corporate identity program in honor of its fifty-fifth anniversary. The cornerstone of the new system is the dynamic blue logo we've all become familiar with. Two features distinguish this mark from others that use a basic oval shape. First, the logo is rotated approximately ten degrees from the x-axis, creating a sense of dynamic tension. Second, the name bleeds out of the mark, visually dissecting it. One can read the outer shape as a spotlight illuminating the brand name.

The National Food Products logo was designed by Jack Gernsheimer in 1994, when NFP was primarily involved in growing, canning, and distributing mushrooms. There were also expressed plans to venture into the handling of additional food products.

As the logo's designer, I struggled with the combination of the three initials. After eliminating the letter P from the equation, the combination of the N and F proved much more workable. Allowing the flag stripe to terminate as a leaf worked effectively from both a conceptual and a visual standpoint.

The colors in the logo were transposed from their use on the U.S. flag because the blend to green worked better from blue than from red. The star, like the letters, was obliqued and reversed to bleed out of the letters, creating unpredictable yet interesting secondary shapes.

The logo for the Dutch municipality of Breda was designed by Kees Zwart in 1994. One can read various images into the mark. The red lines split with white spaces could be seen as three intersections within an active city. Alternatively, they could be seen as three x's in a shieldlike configuration, which is similar to the seal stamped in red wax by the city's noblemen in the Middle Ages.

This updated symbol retains a touch of the old in its outer shape, while it assures modernity with its contemporary appeal. The overall heart shape, whether intentional or not, adds a warm and welcoming spirit.

1994

1995

Federal Express

Creative Circus

The FedEx logo was designed in 1994 by
Lindon Leader at Landor. FedEx capitalized on
the increasing use of the nickname for the
company originally known as Federal Express.
In doing so, they created a customized version
of Futura Black, while retaining the familiar
purple-and-orange color palette. The discreet
treatment of the arrow formed by the negative
space between the *E* and *x* avoided negative
implications when the truck was seen on the
driver's side with the arrow facing backwards.
Sorry, but once you know the arrow is there,
you can never again look at the logo without
seeing it.

The Creative Circus logo designed by
Roger Sawmill and Mark Braught in 1995 uses
fundamental geometric shapes, yet gives
them an implied sense of dimension. The basic
five-pointed star appears to be applied to a
spherical surface, as does the circle in which it
resides. The crimping of the negative spaces
and curving of the star's legs combine to give
the illusion of three-dimensionality. What's
more, the mark requires no gradient shading to
support the spherical appearance. The letter *C*
is present in both positive and negative areas,
adding another layer of relevance by including
both initials, albeit in an understated way. Restraint played an important role in the creation
of this exemplary logo, which represents a
communications art, photo, and design school
in Atlanta.

1995

1997

ca. 1997

Libertel

The Libertel logo was designed by VBAT in 1995. In a manner surprisingly similar to the 1992 logo of leaping dolphins for Danish mobile phone network Sonofon, this logo for the Dutch mobile phone network adopts what appears to be a pair of leaping fish as its logo. Also following Sonofon's lead, the larger Libertel fish or fishlike wave accommodates a smaller dolphin in the negative space.

InXight

The InXight logo, designed by Hyperlink in 1997 and modified in 2002 by MetaDesign, shows how much dimension can be implied in a two-dimensional symbol. Arrows are among the most overused of all graphic elements, yet in this case they are treated freshly and most dynamically. The X created by their convergence reinforces the software company's name and strongly suggests a sense of energy and excitement.

Levi's

Levi Strauss & Company has taken the red tag seen on backsides the world over and appropriated it for its logo. The extreme vertical format helps give distinctiveness and aids in quick recognition, and the red color associates the logo with the valuable brand. Even the stacked letters in the name serve to reinforce brand recognition, while the half "®" cleverly implies the folding of the tag.

ca. 1998

1999

Veer

AIGA

Veer takes good advantage of a short and sweet name, using a friendly cursive font for its signature. Because of its neutrality and agelessness, the type should not need to be replaced over the years. The orange box is anything but incidental. Without it, the logo for this font and image library is little more than a commonplace script. With it, the mark has presence, strength, and rapid recognition. (Just look at it in the URL field of *www.veer.com* to see for yourself.)

The AIGA logo designed in 1999 by Bart Crosby and Gosia Sobus is comfortably surrounded by a box of color, giving it more presence than stand-alone letters. Because of the symmetry and stability of the square, the obliqued type looks progressive, not precariously unbalanced. The classical nature of the perfect square insures longevity, and the extensive color palette, because of its use of mid- to dark-value tones, doesn't overwhelm the delicate and refined type. The customized letters, which appear to be influenced by Galliard Italic, were originally designed by Paul Rand and were refined and strengthened by Crosby Associates. The sharp serifs add a classical, enduring sense, with their chiseled appearance reminiscent of letters carved into stone in the Roman era. This quality is counterbalanced by the highly contemporary nature of the italic caps.

Citi

1999

The Citi logo designed by Pentagram in 1999 capitalizes on the serendipitous presence of the lowercase letter *t* that resembles an umbrella handle. The top of the famed red umbrella, which migrated to Citi when they acquired Travelers, is distilled to a simple red arc. Paula Scher, a partner at Pentagram, recalls drawing a sketch "in one second" on a napkin at an early meeting; that sketch then went on to become the basis for the new symbol. The retention of concept and equity from the early Travelers umbrella, along with the selection of simple, enduring letters, will keep this mark fresh and effective until a name change renders it obsolete.

ca. 1999

Delta Faucets

The Delta Faucets logo has for its fundamental element a water-drop shape. When repeated around an axis three times at 120-degree rotation, a triangle is formed. Delta is the fourth letter in the Greek alphabet and takes its name from the shape of the sediment formation at the mouth of a river. The triangular configuration of the drops set in a circle adds relevance to the logo.

1999

Experimeds

The Experimeds logo was designed by Chris Werner in 1999. The company offered developmental data on prereleased medications via the Internet. Two capsules in a commonly used peel-back package are immediately apparent. What's less apparent is the inclusion of the letter *E* in green on the bottom left and the letter *M* in blue on the upper right. This symbol is an example of imagery that often emerges long after the viewer's first encounter, if at all. As a result, the mark holds a surprise that contains information relevant to the company it represents. The radiused corners add friendliness, and the diamond silhouette has classical simplicity.

H&R BLOCK

2000

ca. 2000

GlaxoSmithKline

The logo for pharmaceutical conglomerate GlaxoSmithKline designed by FutureBrand in 2000 utilizes a radiused triangular profile to give the symbol novelty and make it easily recognizable. Unlike many logos, this mark makes no apologies for its unusual orientation. While there's no specific shape, form, or size to medicine, this configuration has an appearance generic enough to be representative of a pill.

The relationship of the overall shape to the three letters within it is unusual due to the pure horizontal baseline that accentuates the nonaligned silhouette. Despite the asymmetry, the internal spaces and shapes are carefully considered and well balanced.

H & R Block

H & R Block uses the green block to represent their company in a most efficient manner. The selection of Pantone® 376, a very distinctive and intense green, facilitates recognition and suggests economic vitality. Even standing alone and out of context, the logo works to reinforce the strength of this brand.

2000

ca. 2000

2001

Symantec

The Symantec logo was designed in 2000 by Hyperlink. The two-dimensional circle takes on its three-dimensional appearance because we see inside the implied sphere. The negative space describes the letter *S*, while the positive shapes—likely serendipitously—create yin and yang, the ultimate symbol of balance and harmony.

Technicolor Digital Cinema

Technicolor Digital Cinema's logo, designed by Siegel+Gale, is a classic example of a symbol that works on many levels. Its three components utilize blends of RGB—the colors red, blue, and green combined to color imagery. The initials *D* and *C* are clearly visible, while the *T* is comprised of all three components combined, giving the mark its inverted triangular shape. The concave shape of the components is reminiscent of parabolic lenses used in optical engineering.

Entech Engineering

The Entech Engineering logo designed for the multifaceted firm by Jack Gernsheimer in 2001 consists of a cube built out of three *E*'s. When placed on a white, black, or red background, two of the three sides are fully visible. The third side is completed by extrapolating visual information given by the other two.

An admittedly serendipitous, yet important, by-product of the letter placement is the secondary suggestion that one can step multidimensionally down, up, or sideways into the cube in Escher-like fashion, suggesting accessibility into a structure. The use of a perfect cube implies aesthetic sensitivity coupled with strength, two qualities desired in the design and construction of structures large and small. The classical cube also ensures that this mark will transcend time and fashion and will endure, if called upon to do so, for decades.

NATIONAL GEOGRAPHIC

ᴎⵏEU 2004

2002

2004

National Geographic

National Geographic takes advantage of tre-
mendous equity by smartly utilizing the yellow
box that has framed its magazine covers for
decades. Designed by Chermayeff and Geismar
around 2002, this most simple of solutions is
actually right on the money. The organization
is figuratively encompassed within the box,
thus adding validity to ventures such as TV
programming that are offshoots of the flagship
product, the venerable magazine.

Dutch EU Presidency

The logo designed by Studio Dumbar for the
Dutch EU Presidency 2004 exemplifies typography that is playful, appealing, and smart. By
turning the *n* and *l* on their side, an elegantly
stylized *E* appears. While the character would
be less identifiable taken out of context, it
reads clearly when combined with the other
components in this colorful cluster. The end
result is a symbol full of positive energy, vitality, and confidence.

01   02   03

SECTION 3 OFFERS THE OPPORTUNITY TO FOLLOW A DESIGNER'S THOUGHT

PROCESS AS DESIGNS EVOLVE, FROM INCEPTION TO COMPLETION. Thanks to

the ease of stepping and repeating, today's designer can create a mark, then copy

and modify it continually, until he feels it is fully developed.

In many cases, you'll see not only the logo design chosen by the client, but also

those marks that were not chosen. There are even designs that, for one reason or

another, were not presented to the client.

ALL STAR DISTRIBUTING

1997	1998	1999	2000	2001

The logo for this beer distribution company designed by Chris Werner in 2002 takes a shape too frequently and indiscriminately used, the five-pointed star. In this case, however, it is both appropriate and highly distinctive, by virtue of the simple yet widely identifiable silhouette of a beer bottle within the star. Because the overall shape is a simple geometric one and the basic beer bottle hasn't changed in many decades, the likelihood of this logo enduring is very strong.

The treatment of the mark is understated and sophisticated, and the blind embossing seen on the business cards works very effectively because the resulting debossed image is also right reading. The same applies to the custom-cut signage, with the added dimension of a half bottle formed by the profile of the sign (see *www.partnersdesign.net/allstar*). This is a good example of two commonly seen objects made special by their interaction. Because of the simplicity of the mark, the size and placement must be carefully considered. As a general rule of thumb, the simpler the mark, the more critical every decision becomes.

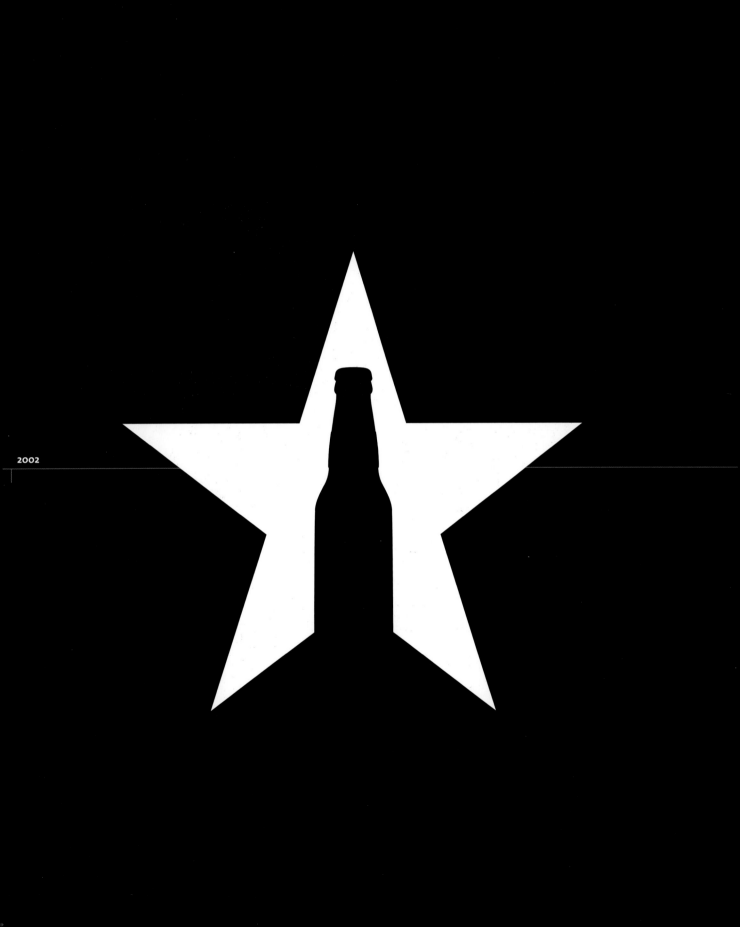

All Star Distributing

Winged Circle

This logo designed by Jack Gernsheimer was inspired by one I did in 2000 for Showcase Station (see page 61); both are reminiscent of commercial signage of the first half of the twentieth century. The wings are somewhat similar to those of the Mobil Oil Pegasus (see page 111) and other gas station graphics commonly seen in that period. As is the case with the oil company logos, this All Star logo imparts a sense of speed and dependability.

When it comes to logos of this genre and period, the rules of classical logo design are relaxed in favor of faithful adherence to the style of the era. While there is appeal for extensive detail and visual activity, there are drawbacks as well. This type of mark is better suited for a small business, such as a retail store or a restaurant, than for a corporation.

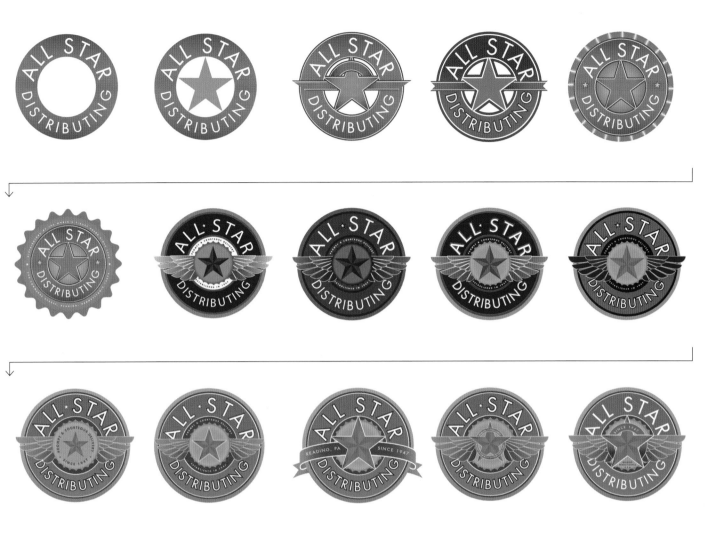

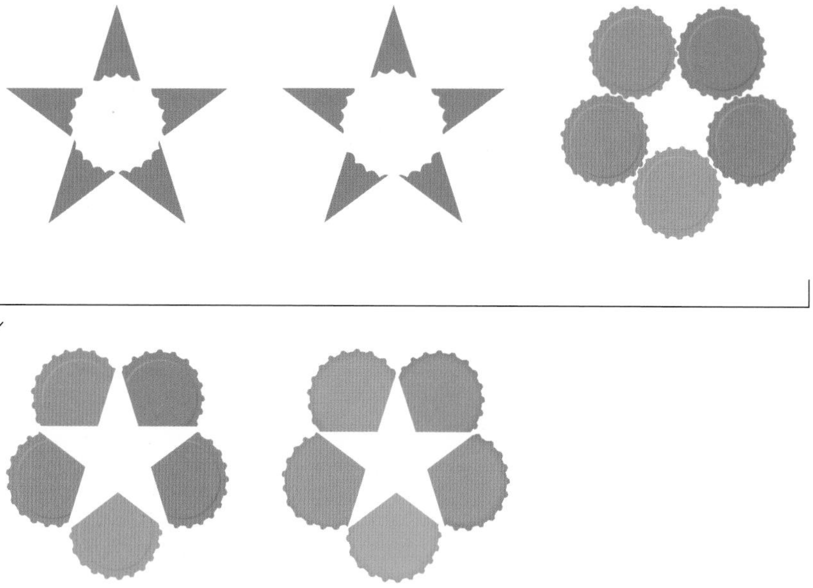

All Star Distributing

Cap Cluster

The varied results of the interaction between the star and the bottle cap(s) are explored in this design. I explored a cap within the star and vice versa. An associate, Sean Costik, explored the clustering of five colored caps, then I looked at varied-sized stars in the center. The multicoloration, though not essential, effectively suggested product variety. Because the colors are very close in value, they give a nearly monochromatic appearance at first glance and hold together well. The outer pentagon shape is pleasing, and the components of this symbol relate thematically to the product.

All Star Distributing

Baseball

There are three elements interacting in this design alternative. The outer bottle cap provides a distinctive silhouette, made more recognizable with highlights and shadows that support the illusion of embossing. The star is viewed both straight up and obliqued, which matches the angle of the script. The name is built with characters modified from the Eclat font because of their baseball-like appearance. The swash beneath the words is influenced by the Brooklyn Dodgers uniform, a look now widely used in baseball and nonbaseball applications alike.

AMERICAN SOCIETY OF PICTURE PROFESSIONALS

A typographic search yielded the Impact font as the top candidate for the American Society of Picture Professionals (ASPP) logo because the characters are clearly defined in spite of the narrow openings created by condensing the negative spaces dramatically. Very few condensed, sans serif fonts have such narrow openings, and those that do tend to have compromised legibility.

Once chosen, the type was converted to outline, and all the characters were modified to create a reflective balance. Serendipity lent a hand, as it often does, because the lowercase *a* and *s* could be modified to pleasingly reflect one another. The ground glass-like center adds both visual interest and relevance. Not only does the circle with its four defined quadrants evoke the mechanism commonly used to assist in focusing the camera, the perfect circle with crosshairs implies a sense of sharp focus in both a physical and procedural sense. As seen in the developmental iterations, the use of cyan, magenta, yellow, and black was considered but yielded to a more primary, less literal color palette. Finally, the concentrated and compressed nature of the mark gives it, and the organization it represents, a sense of cohesiveness and strength.

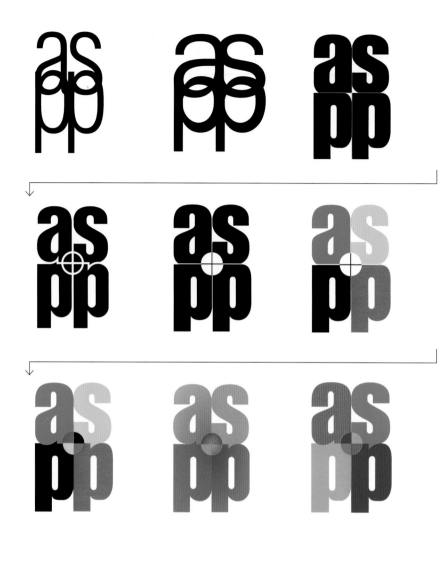

American Society of Picture Professionals

Final Evolution

American Society of Picture Professionals

Letters

The second exploration again makes the letters the prominent feature; that often makes sense when dealing with an acronym or short name. Essentially, the concept is handed to you because logotypes using a small number of letters can render a symbol redundant and superfluous. Not only do the characters potentially interact well, they are more direct than many symbols. While cases like CBS exemplify the successful union of initials and a symbol, ABC makes a strong case against the need for an accompanying mark.

In this exploration, serif characters give way to bold sans serifs. The tight crop plays with the idea of image cropping and makes the characters more novel and dynamic.

BERKS COUNTY COMMUNITY FOUNDATION

2001   2002   2003   2004   2005

The version of the Berks County Community Foundation (BCCF) logo selected by the client involves the diamond shape in both the basic units and outer silhouette. The mark was designed by Chris Werner and Jeff Gernsheimer in 2006. Clearly represented are a set of steps implying growth and momentum. Projecting the sun on the step surfaces adds a sense of brightness and hope, feelings experienced by the recipients of the many charitable funds distributed by the organization. The rays increase in number as they move away from the viewer, adding visual interest and a greater sense of dimension, as do the gradient colors within the rays.

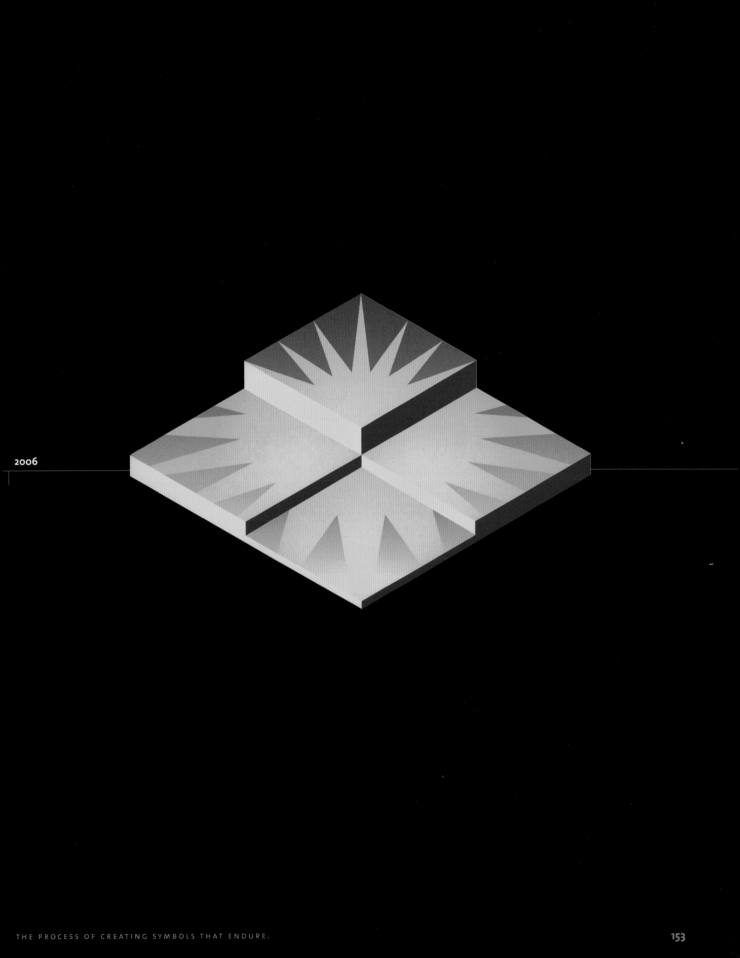

Berks County Community Foundation

Pentagon

The humanlike figures clustered in a five-star configuration give this symbol a sense of cohesive co-operation. The appendages give a secondary impression of leaves, suggesting growth. The inclusion of the heart, while often cliché, seems less so here because of its integration into the overall mark, where it adds a dimension of warmth and sensitivity.

While not an essential component of this logo, gradient color is used to support the imagery, helping to define both the central heart and the leaves. The outer shape of the mark is a pentagon, a polygon used less frequently than the square, circle, or triangle, thus giving it a more distinctive and stable, yet classical, silhouette.

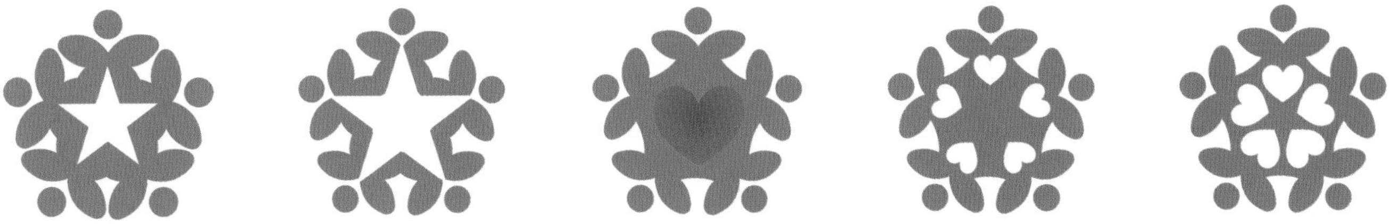

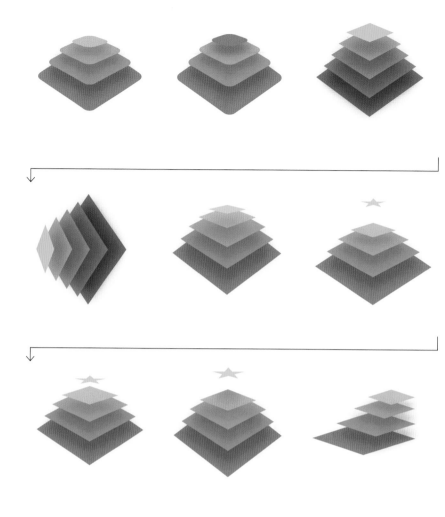

Berks County Community Foundation

Pagoda

The first exploration shows the development of a pagoda-like icon. Originally conceived as a set of steps, the mark was meant to suggest treading upward. The mark's similarity to an Eastern temple was relevant because a pagoda stands atop a hill overlooking Reading, the heart of Berks County, Pennsylvania. Additionally, the county is shaped like a diamond, as was the logo's silhouette, adding a layer of secondary information. The colors brightened as they moved upward, suggesting an uplifting spirit for this philanthropic organization.

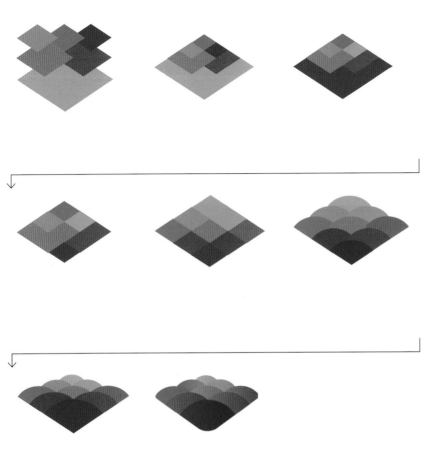

Berks County Community Foundation

Fields

The second exploration again takes the diamond as the basic unit and evolves to a point where the outer shape is diamond-like, as well. Unlike the first design, this version does not step upward; rather, it takes on the appearance of a patchwork quilt of deeply saturated colors. As the design develops, the basic units acquire roundness as well as perspective, giving the concluding mark a softness as well as a distinctive appearance suggestive of the rolling hills of the region. While agriculture plays a less-prominent role in the community than it previously did, it is still an important part of the local heritage.

BODYFIT

The BodyFit logo, created by Jack Gernsheimer in 1996 for a manufacturer of fitness apparatus, incorporates an Atlas-like figure triumphantly raising the globe above his head. The sprocket motif gives the symbol an industrial look reminiscent of the Constructivist period following World War I, and the stylization of the human figure and globe convey a utilitarian quality inherent in the products.

In keeping with the symmetrical structure, the product line name "BodyFit" is reinforced by the reflective message "Fit Body." The playful twist of the phrase "Work Hard. Play Hard." to "Work Hard. Stay Hard." allows the beholder to interpret the message in a number of ways. The reverse treatment of black and white from side to side is established initially to suggest hemispheric time change on the globe, and it emanates into the typography and border motif. The sprocket activity adds a degree of visual interest and an underlying suggestion of functionality, quality, and strength.

WORK HARD
STAY HARD™
FIT™
FIT™
BODY
BODY
1996

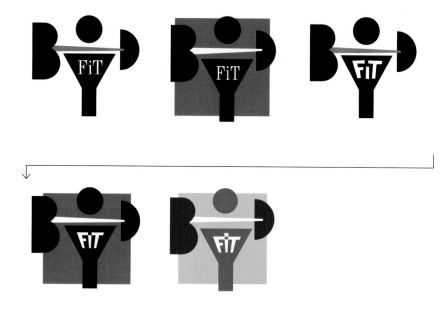

BodyFit

Weight Lifter

The version shown here explores the use of the four
letters in the word "body." The characters are handled
in a playful, nonlinear form. The letters *B* and *D* become
weights on a bar. The letter *O* represents the lifter's head,
and the *Y* is the body. The customized word "fit," while
resembling the treatment of the word "body," emblazons
the figure's "chest" as if on a T-shirt.

    This mark illustrates that serendipitous imagery
often waits to be revealed when the logo exploration process begins, provided the designer is open to unexpected
revelations. The primary colors add levity and longevity to
the symbol, and the yellow square helps hold it together.
Allowing the characters to violate the square adds dimension and presence as well as visual interest.

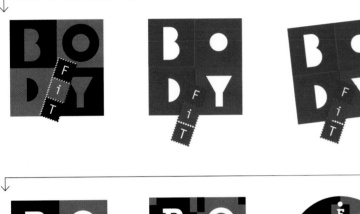

BodyFit

Four Square

This design alternative capitalizes on the fact that both words in the company name are short, which makes them generally easier to work with than long words. In this case, the four letters stack two on two, and the word "fit" interacts playfully with the word "body." The letters themselves appear to be punched out of the boxes as if they were stencils, and the shapes are greatly simplified. The checkerboard look gives added distinctiveness.

The shortcoming of this version is the use of the playful logo style and its inappropriateness to the product. This design pursuit illustrates the important point that we can become seduced by visual appeal. It's important to step back occasionally and ask yourself if this solution is well founded or invalid. If it is the latter, resist the urge to submit it, because if selected, it will not serve the client well. The quality of submissions is always more important than the quantity.

BodyFit

Final Version

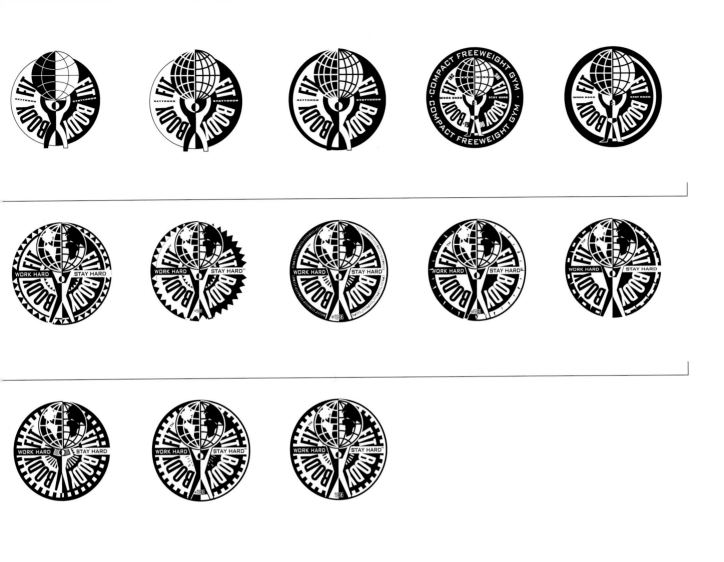

CARPENTER TECHNOLOGY CORPORATION

1991	1992	1993	1994	1995

The Carpenter Technology Corporation logo was designed by Jack Gernsheimer in 1996. The century-old company's primary product is specialty steel used in many industrial sectors, such as aeronautics, automotive, and medical.

The logo was inspired by the red-hot coil of steel wire (see page 34) resulting from the process of heating and lengthening an ingot of steel. As the metal is stretched, it becomes longer and thinner until it is as thin as wire, at which time it is coiled and cooled.

Within the logo, a short and thick letter *C*, with a 240-degree circumference, is the center-most element representing the ingot or thickest state of the steel. As additional *C*'s emanate concentrically outward, they rotate counterclockwise sixty degrees and become thinner and longer, as does the wire.

When seen at a reduced size, the overall shape of the logo is also that of the letter *C*, as is the resulting negative space. Added visual activity results from the increasing width of the spaces between *C*'s as the letters become longer and thinner.

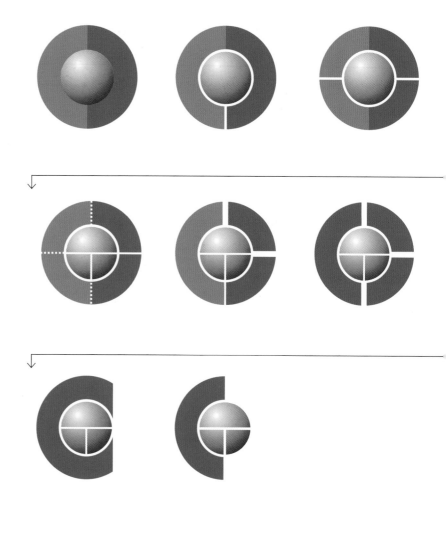

Carpenter

Steel Balls

This alternative for the Carpenter logo recognizes that at the core of the company's operations, there is steel. The center sphere has a highlight and shading, giving it the look of a ball bearing. Encasing the central element are various quarter and half circles that resemble the letter *C* when spacing and color are applied. The letter *T* appears in various forms, as well.

The circular shape keeps the mark nicely self-contained. One potential problem exists due to the dependence on using a gradient to imply dimension. The gradient could sometimes, although not often, be difficult to reproduce. By the same token, imagine how attractive a half sphere of steel would look emerging from a conference-room wall.

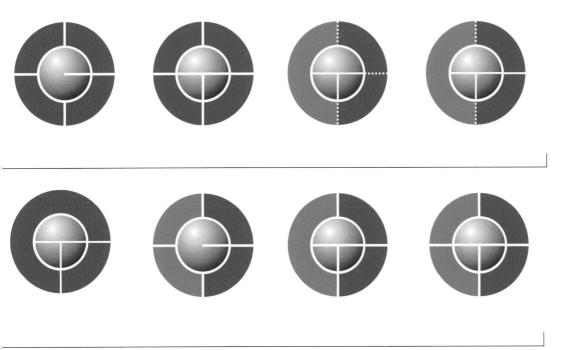

Carpenter

Galaxy

In this extensive exploration, the initial versions include rules going around a central point in a circular fashion. The longest and thinnest line is placed at three o'clock. Moving clockwise, each line is shorter and thicker, creating a nautilus-like symbol. There is a circular opening in the center, giving the element a *C*-like shape. Because of the thickening lines at the top of the mark, a secondary *C* can be detected. This mark is arguably as strong and distinctive as the logo that was finally chosen. The same stretching and thinning concept applies, substituting rods for coils. Further exploration included skewing the mark, and giving it a galaxy-like and Saturn-like appearance.

As the designer, I had lingering concerns about similarity to the United Technologies logo (see page 120). In the end, I was advised to abandon the design for that reason.

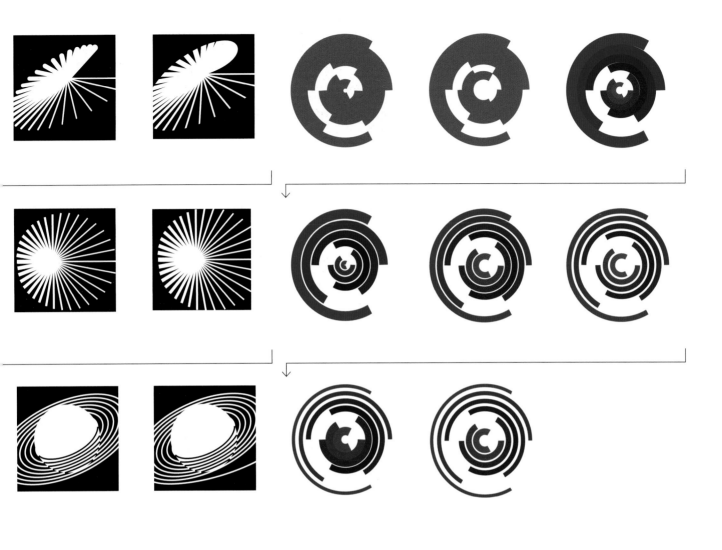

Carpenter

Alternate Final Development

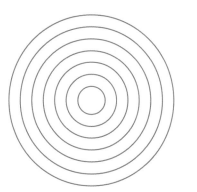

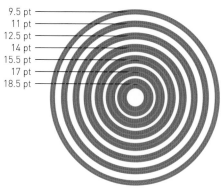

9.5 pt
11 pt
12.5 pt
14 pt
15.5 pt
17 pt
18.5 pt

Carpenter

Logo Construction

The construction of the Carpenter Technology logo begins with seven equally spaced concentric circles. The circles are then given a line thickness, with the thinnest on the outside and the thickest on the inside. As the lines thicken, the space between the lines thins, adding visual interest to the symbol. The lines are then cut and rotated as shown.

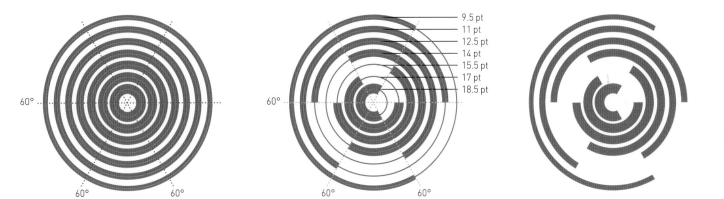

DUTCH GOLD HONEY

1997	1998	1999	2000	2001

The Dutch Gold Honey logo, designed by Jack Gernsheimer in 2002, is the result of the interaction between six hexagons overlapping a six-pointed rosette.

The hexagonal cluster represents the honeycomb, where the honey is collected. The rosette is a common component of hex signs, which are seen in the region where the company is located, known as Pennsylvania Dutch country. According to local lore, the six-pointed rosette is believed to ward off evil and bad luck.

The overall floral quality of the logo gives added relevance to the mark because pollen, collected by bees from flowers, is an essential part of the honey-making process. The clustered element holds together well, is self-contained, and has a distinctive silhouette for quicker recognition.

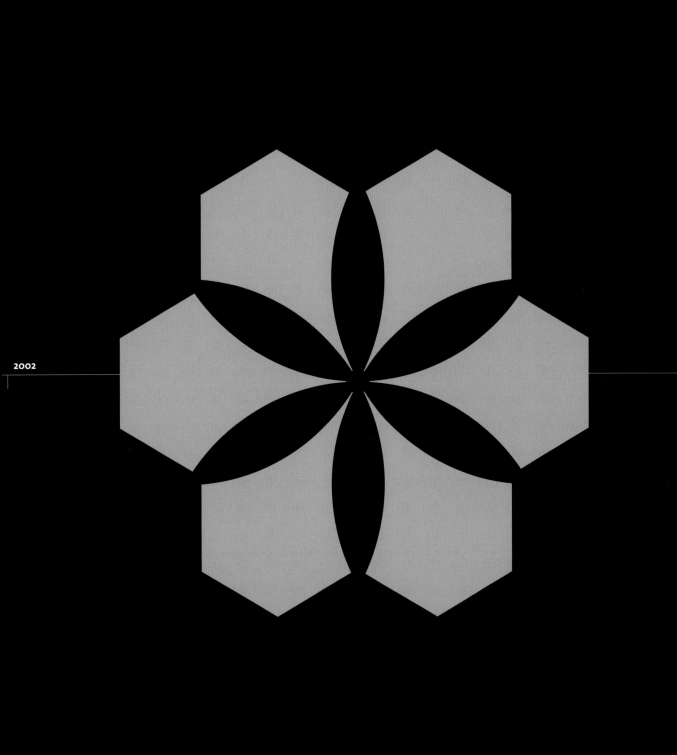

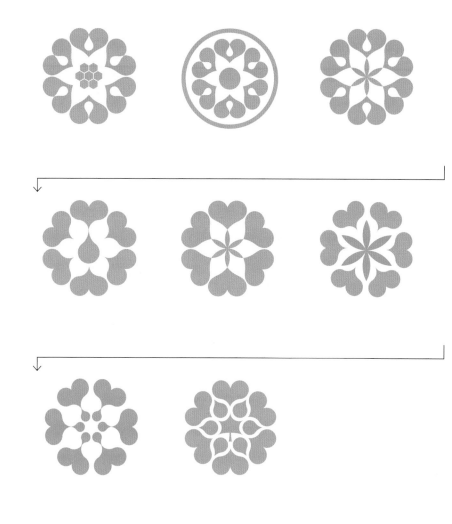

Dutch Gold Honey / McClure's Maple Syrup

Hearts and Drops

This alternative looks at hex sign–like designs combining stylized hearts, drops of honey or syrup, and flower petals in the negative space. These symbols layer in a lot of relevant imagery, but order is kept because they are arranged in a circular configuration and have a well-balanced ratio of positive to negative space. The hearts support the idea that both the syrup and the honey qualify as comfort food, while the hex elements give the mark a clear sense of local color.

Dutch Gold Honey

Chosen Alternative Exploration

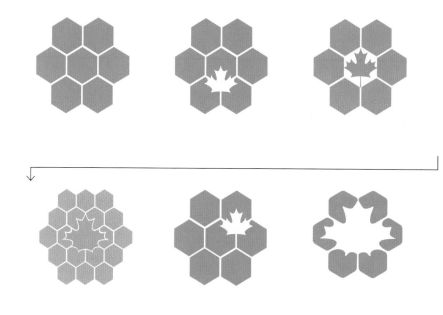

McClure's Maple Syrup

Concurrent Exploration

While the Dutch Gold Honey logo was being designed, a concurrent exploration was being pursued. Because DGH is the parent company of McClure's Maple Syrup, this alternative explored the use of imagery relevant to both honey and syrup. Various degrees of interaction between the cluster of hexagons and a stylized maple leaf silhouette were observed. Arguably the most successful symbol was the alternative that placed the large leaf in the center, creating a pleasing symmetry. The rounded shapes added warmth and softness to the overall mark.

Shown on the right is a close-up of the embossed logo on the front and back panels of the plastic honey jar.

LENTZ MILLING COMPANY

The Lentz logo, designed in 2006 by Jack Gernsheimer for a distributor of baking-related products, began innocently enough with an eight-pointed star in the negative space that was created by the forty-five degree rotation of eight *L*'s. As the design progressed, the letter *M* emerged as the *L*'s rotated, albeit somewhat obscurely. Further observation and development brought the transformation of the letters into stylized stalks of grain, and from that point on scores of variations on that theme were explored. Numerous alternatives were reviewed because of concerns regarding the negative space appearing too prominent and the symbol too closely resembling a snowflake. With further exploration came the virtual disappearance of the letter *M*, determined a nonessential component and one that added unnecessary activity and confusion. Roughening the texture of the symbol helped assuage concerns about the lack of original appearance.

Inherent in many of the design alternatives is the compass, symbolizing the distribution of product. Also emerging in the negative space were various shapes resembling clusters of grain.

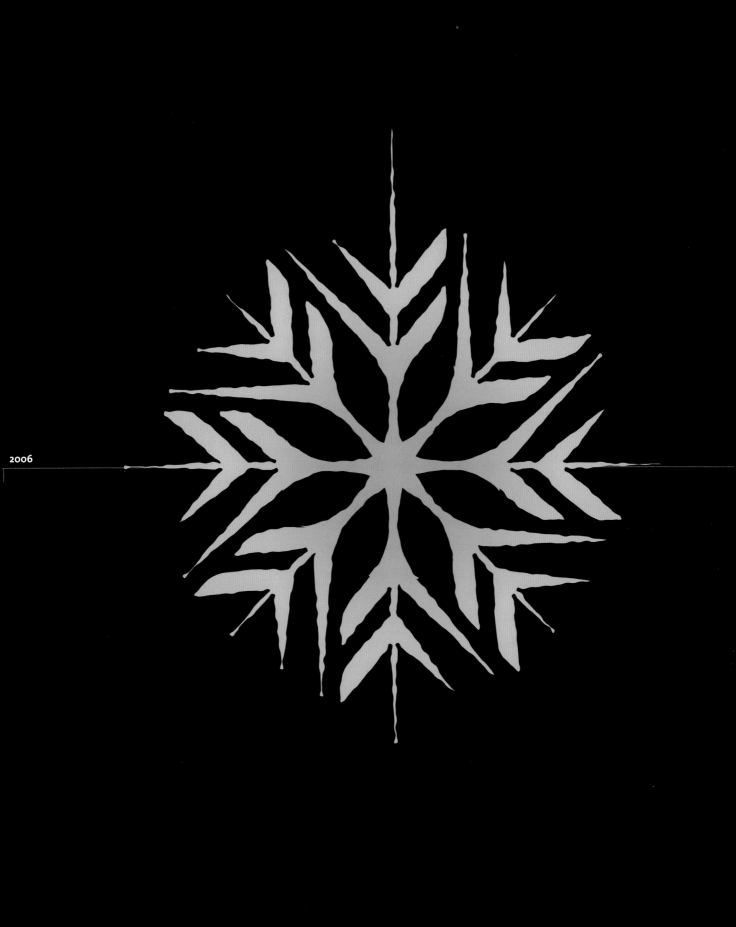

2006

Lentz Milling Company

Explorations

Lentz Milling Company

Explorations

PICTURE ARCHIVE COUNCIL OF AMERICA

1998   1999   2000   2001   2002

The PACA logo consists of the letters *P*, *A*, *C*, and *A*, which interweave to create a cohesive element. Although custom designed, the letters are reminiscent of lowercase Futura characters, selected because of their pure circular form. They are stacked two atop two, forming a square, and are contained in a square black box. The use of these pure geometric shapes helps give this simple mark a classical quality.

The interweaving circular elements, while adding implied dimension, are suggestive of the aperture of a camera's lens. They also support the idea that combining forces results in increased strength. The varied colors of the letters suggest diversity, which exists in both PACA's membership and in the variety of images and libraries represented.

Picture Archive Council of America

Alternative Exploration

The uppercase alternative design for the PACA again explores the stacking of two letters on two letters. The negative spaces between the letters take on interesting secondary shapes. The squaring off of the spaces inside the letters *P* and *A* gives the letters a distinctive quality, and the bold characters suggest strength and solidity. Additional linear configuration alternatives explore how the letters work on one line, both overlapped and not overlapped. The slightly smoky color tones add to the appeal of this design.

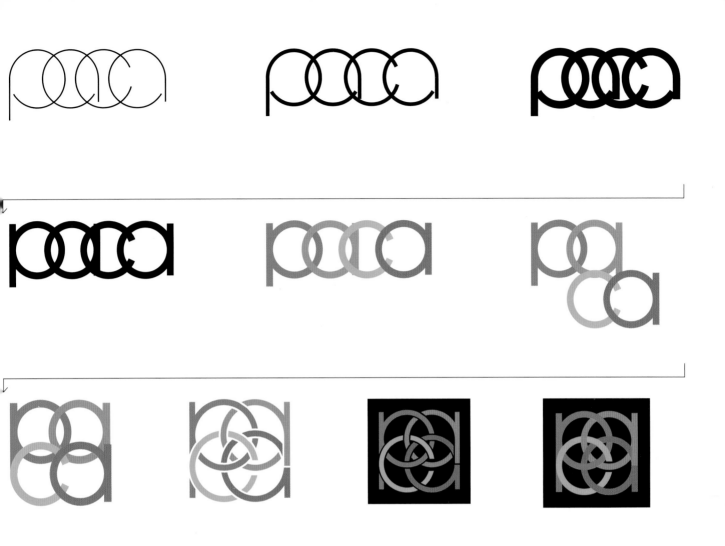

Picture Archive Council of America

Design Evolution

THE PICTURE DESK

2001   2002   2003   2004   2005

The Picture Desk is a London-based stock image archive containing two collections. Logos for The Art Archive (TAA) and The Kobal Collection (TKC), as well as The Picture Desk (TPD), were designed in 2006 by Jack Gernsheimer. As the designer, I began the logo design process by observing logo alternatives for the parent company (TPD). A number of initial options were explored, some of which were developed in tandem with TAA and TKC. A breakthrough happened when obvious imagery emerged. Because The Kobal Collection pertained to movies, TV, and entertainment, I decided to represent the letter *O* as a searchlight. Once that was developed, the pyramid eventually followed, due to the historical, civilizational, and artistic imagery of The Art Archive.

Other techniques employed to unify the two identities included dividing the background into quadrants with gradients to enrich the two nearly monochromatic palettes. Also, there is light emanating from within both logos.

The Picture Desk

Little Table

This design alternative plays directly off the name "The Picture Desk." The desk is reduced to a small square-topped table with what appear to be picture frames sitting on the surface. Gray values and shadows help define the objects and imply three-dimensionality. The frames take on added significance when they take the shape of a lowercase *p* and *d*. In a later version, the circular type treatment envelops the symbol and accommodates additional identifying information. Also, color rather than value defines the surfaces of the desk and frames. With or without the circle, the elements hold together and the mark is cohesive. There is a solidity and time-neutral quality because of the thickness and simplicity of the components. The weight also makes reduction more successful.

The Picture Desk

Retro

This alternative takes a totally different approach to the design of The Picture Desk logo. The mark evokes a spirit of a bygone era and incorporates imagery relevant to the archive it represents. The movie reel, though long since replaced with a string of technologically advanced media, is still a recognizable icon within the entertainment industry. The artist's brushes and palette support the idea that TAA provides art-related imagery. The integration of primary and secondary type gives additional informa-tion and adds visual appeal. The name "Picture Desk" is custom designed and appears to be on a concave surface, thus adding distinctiveness and dimension.

The Picture Desk

Brackets

These versions of the three group logos—TKC, TAA, and TPD—look at various ways of accommodating the key word, which is dropped out to white within the colored rectangle. These treatments are intended to be used as logotypes more than as self-sufficient symbols. The shape represents a picture in the collection, and it is shown first with brackets partially framing the image. Next, the shape appears to be held by slits in the paper. This version is then taken a step further by suggesting that a translucent stock is being used. The final version shows one of the four images not yet in place, implying that this is a work in progress.

This group of alternatives is unlikely to be used without accompanying words. They coordinate well with one another and in fact are even more effective as a group than when treated independently.

THE ART ARCHIVE

THE KOBAL COLLECTION

The Picture Desk

Final Evolution

THE PLUMBING WORKS

The Plumbing Works logo designed in 2004 by Jack Gernsheimer was not the mark ultimately chosen by the client. This logo combines a silhouette of a vertical pipe with water flowing freely from a faucet. Various degrees of detail are explored to determine how literal or stylized the profile should be. The juxtaposition of the complex detail of the spigot combined with the simplified stylization of the flowing water is interesting but somewhat contradictory. That contradiction suggests further exploration, with simplification of the mechanical unit more closely reflecting the stylization of the flowing water.

The letters inherent in the mark are *t, p,* and *w.* Further observation compares various details in order to arrive at a version that retains legibility and compatibility of the individual characters yet clearly illustrates the components.

The Plumbing Works

The Chosen Version

The selected version designed by Sean Costik adhered more closely to the predetermined objective of developing a logotype that took advantage of their small fleet of trucks as rolling billboards. The letter *w* suggests a pipe that is open, allowing water to flow freely through it. The strong color palette of red, white, and black makes the trucks highly visible and memorable, while it suggests confidence as well as competence. The letters are softened to add a degree of friendliness, which also implies good service.

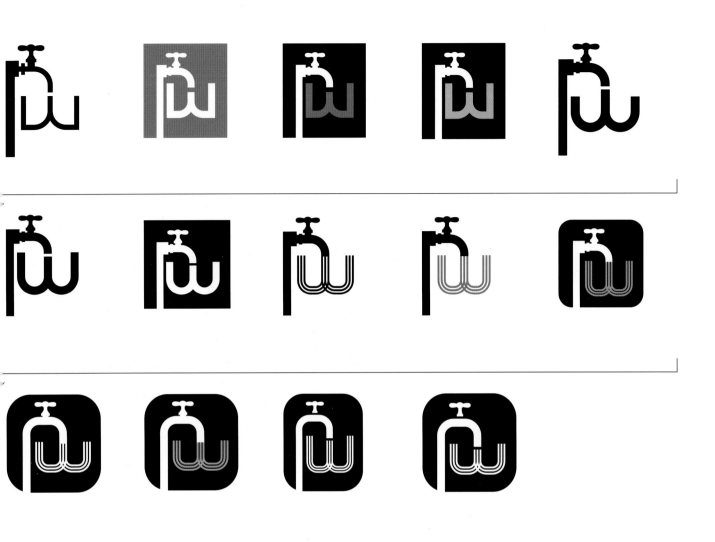

THE IMAGE WORKS

2001   2002   2003   2004   2005

The Image Works and Stockphotos.com logos and logotypes were designed by Jack Gernsheimer in 2006. A primary objective of the identity revamp was to create a look that visually tied together the two divisions of this editorial photo archive.

Starting with Helvetica Bold Condensed characters, most letters were customized to interact pleasingly with their neighbors and friends. The combination of capped and lowercase letters, while not unique, was used to eliminate ascenders and descenders. In doing so, the space between words, known as leading, could be tightened. This created a stack of words cohesively knit together. The Bauhaus-like *m* and *w* added distinctiveness and interacted well with one another.

The stacks were justified by manipulating the size, shape, and spacing of the individual letters, as well as the sizing of the accompanying stamp. The key word was emphasized by reducing the grayscale value of the secondary words. In the case of the Image Works, the verbal double entendre adds a playful touch, as does the interchanging of caps and lowercase characters.

The Image Works

Stamp Version

The stamp element, consisting of a stylized *T*, *I*, and *W*, has a pleasingly symmetrical appearance which is made more organic and interesting by virtue of its distressed, stamplike texture. The mark has a smiling nature, adding friendliness to a logo that represents a highly skilled, helpful, and pleasant group of photo archivists. The line weight of the stamp is designed to work well with that of the letters.

Amusingly, more than one party offered to "clean up" the broken logo before it went to print, making a strong case for providing a standards sheet—also referred to as a style sheet—to vendors and suppliers. During the developmental process, cocking the stamp was considered, but ultimately rejected, as a way of reinforcing the stamplike broken image quality.

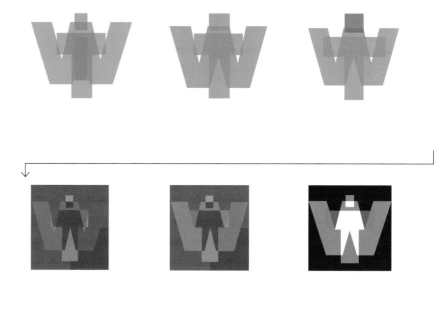

The Image Works

Overlap Version

This design exploration began with the overlapping of the letters *T*, *I*, and *W*. Initially, it looked hard to read, but when the letters became less opaque, a humanlike body could be detected. Reducing the dot of the lowercase *i* gave the body a head. Taking the color out of the figure helped define it and made it more easily visible. One version had the figure holding a camera, but that added more detail and less clarity, so an earlier iteration became the presented version. Retaining the steps allowed for backtracking when the exploration had gone too far.

The Image Works

Books Version

This design alternative is based on the fact that Image Works deals primarily with editorial rather than commercial image usage. The fanning pages appear and suggest that this is a magazine or book. The configuration of the elements creates a stylized letter *W* for "Works." This mark has a sense of balance, dimension, and visual appeal, but it's conceptually vague and doesn't relate directly enough to the client. Had it been designed for a publication about Volkswagens, it would have been great.

THE MAIN COURSE

2002	2003	2004	2005	2006

Designed in 2007 by Jack Gernsheimer, this Main Course logo alternative, although not the one finally chosen, intrigued the client greatly and spawned extensive exploration. Each of the three initials became an integral part of the illustration, as did the negative space. The letter *T* tops the image as a chef's hat. Moving down the figure, the letter *M* becomes the upper body of the chef, creating negative space that represents the head down to the open collar of the white jacket. The letter *C* evolved from a platter with a lid, or nondescript shape, to the clear though subtle representation of a fish being presented to the viewer. The repetitive use of small circles to suggest the chef's eye, the jacket's buttons, and the fish's eye adds continuity as well as a stylistic element that helps define the objects. The segmented background adds color and personality to the symbol, as does the face divided by color and value.

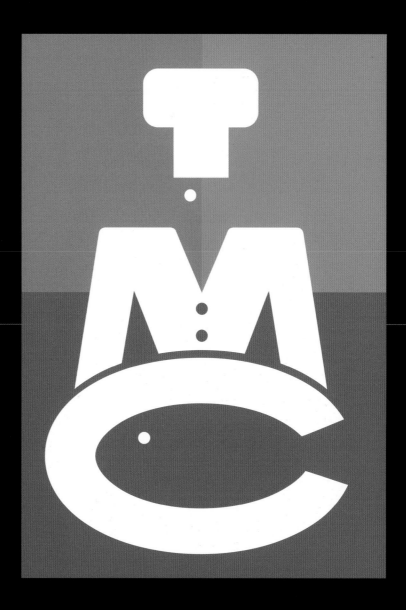

The Main Course

Chosen Version

In the end, when the final logo was selected, it was decided that while the chef mark was clever and appealing, it would have been more appropriate for a catering service or a restaurant specializing in seafood rather than a meal-preparation facility. The selected mark designed by Chris Werner in 2007 utilizes objects that provide scale to one another. The spoon handle in particular suggests that this is a mixing bowl, thus implying that the portion within the bowl is large. The handle of the lid also adds scale to the objects. The line beneath the rim of the bowl reflects that of the base of the lid sitting atop a serving platter. There is a sense of sequence at play as well, with the preparation phase seen above and the presentation phase seen below. The directness, simplicity, and period neutrality of this symbol ensure that the logo will be appropriate and will clearly communicate for decades.

INDEX

BOOKS FROM ALLWORTH PRESS

How to Think Like a Graphic Designer
by Debbie Millman (6 × 9, 256 pages, paperback, $24.95)

The Elements of Graphic Design: Space, Unity, Page Architecture, and Type
by Alex W. White (6⅛ × 9¼, 160 pages, 350 b&w illustrations, paperback, $24.95)

Thinking in Type: The Practical Philosophy of Typography
by Alex W. White (6 × 9, 224 pages, paperback, $24.95)

The Graphic Designer's Guide to Better Business Writing
by Barbara Janoff and Ruth Cash-Smith (6 × 9, 256 pages, paperback, $19.95)

The Graphic Design Business Book
by Tad Crawford (6 × 9, 256 pages, paperback, $24.95)

The Graphic Designer's Guide to Pricing, Estimating, and Budgeting, Revised Edition
by Theo Stephan Williams (6¾ × 9⅞, 208 pages, paperback, $19.95)

How to Grow as a Graphic Designer
by Catharine Fishel (6 × 9, 256 pages, paperback, $19.95)

AIGA Professional Practices in Graphic Design, Second Edition
Edited by Tad Crawford (6 × 9, 320 pages, paperback, $29.95)

Design Management: Using Design to Build Brand Value and Corporate Innovation
by Brigitte Borja de Mozota (6 × 9, 256 pages, paperback, $24.95)

Business and Legal Forms for Graphic Designers, Third Edition
by Tad Crawford and Eva Doman Bruck (8½ × 11, 208 pages, paperback, includes CD-ROM, $35.00)

Creating the Perfect Design Brief: How to Manage Design for Strategic Advantage
by Peter L. Philips (6 × 9, 224 pages, paperback, $19.95)

Advertising Design and Typography
by Alex W. White (8¾ × 11¼, 224 pages, 1500 color illustrations, hardcover, $50.00)

The Graphic Designer's Guide to Clients: How to Make Clients Happy and Do Great Work
by Ellen Shapiro (6 × 9, 256 pages, paperback, $19.95)

To request a free catalog or order books by credit card, call 1-800-491-2808. To see our complete catalog on the World Wide Web, or to order online for a 20 percent discount, you can find us at *www.allworth.com*.